Creating
High Performance
Organizations

Creating High Performance Organizations

*Practices and Results
of Employee Involvement
and Total Quality Management
in Fortune 1000 Companies*

Edward E. Lawler III

Susan Albers Mohrman

Gerald E. Ledford, Jr.

A Study Commissioned by
the Association for Quality and Participation

Jossey-Bass Publishers

San Francisco

Substantial discounts on bulk quantities of Jossey-Bass books are available to corporations, professional associations, and other organizations. For details and discount information, contact the special sales department at Jossey-Bass, Inc., Publisners. (415) 433-1740. Fax (800) 605-2665.

For sales outside the United States, please contact your local Paramount Publishing International Office.

Printed on acid-free paper and manufactured in the United States of America.

Produced by *Publishing Professionals*, Eugene, Oregon.

Cover and interior design by Mark Ong, *Side by Side Studios*.

Library of Congress Cataloging-in-Publication Data

Lawler, Edward E.
  Creating high performance organizations : practices and results of employee involvement
and total quality management in Fortune 1000 companies /
E. Lawler III, Susan A. Mohrman, Gerald E. Ledford, Jr.
    P.   cm. — (The Jossey-Bass management series)
  Includes bibliographical references.
  ISBN 0-7879-0171-7 (alk. paper)
  1. Total quality management—United States. 2. Management–
Employee participation. 3. Industrial productivity–
United States. 4. Employer attitude surveys–United States.
I. Mohrman, Susan Albers. II. Ledford, Gerald E., Jr. III Title.
IV. Series.
HD62. 15.L39 1995
  658.5′ 62—dc20   95-9136
                                                                           CIP

FIRST EDITION
PB Printing   10 9 8 7 6 5 4 3 2 1

The Jossey-Bass
Management Series

Contents

Tables
and Figures

Preface

Organizational effectiveness is an increasingly popular topic in the management literature. Proponents argue that it is the key to gaining competitive advantage in today's highly competitive business environment. Employee involvement and total quality management are frequently mentioned approaches to improving organizational effectiveness. Our interest in employee involvement dates back decades and includes a considerable amount of research, as well as consulting. Despite great interest in the topic and a great deal of research, little systematic information exists on why companies are adopting employee involvement programs, what types of practices they are using as part of their employee involvement programs, how effective they think employee involvement is, and how effective it actually is. Much the same is true for total quality management. Widespread interest in it is more recent but nevertheless pervasive. In many organizations, total quality management is closely related to employee involvement; thus, studying one without the other is ill advised.

Creating High Performance Organizations represents the third phase of a long-term research program aimed at documenting how management practices in Fortune 1000 corporations are changing. The first phase involved a 1987 survey that focused on which types of employee involvement practices were being adopted by Fortune 1000 corporations and on their views of the effectiveness of these practices (Lawler, Ledford, and Mohrman, 1989). The second phase involved a 1990 follow-up survey of the Fortune 1000 (Lawler, Mohrman and Ledford, 1992). A comparison of the 1987 and 1990 data showed changes over time in the adoption rate for employee involvement practices among large U.S. firms. It also provided a benchmark of the degree to which employee involvement practices are actually utilized by U.S. corporations.

The present study extends these analyses to 1993 and provides much more extensive data on who adopts total quality management and what the results are. This information is very appropriate and important given the central role total quality management has in the efforts of many organizations to improve their performance.

In the earlier studies, only the impact of employee involvement and total quality management on nonfinancial performance measures was considered, whereas the present one includes their effect on such financial results as return on equity. In addition, this study provides important new systematic data on what is happening with respect to management trends in the United States. Overall this study presents an interesting story of increased utilization of both employee involvement and total quality management and a report of their effectiveness.

The information we present should be of use to managers who are considering changing their management approach and to researchers who are in search of data on how management practices are changing in the United States. Managers who wish to compare their own organization change efforts can use the data to measure their own organizations against those of the Fortune 1000.

We also look at the relationship between the employee involvement and total quality management practices. These results should be especially helpful to managers and researchers interested in the separate and joint impact of total quality management practices and employee involvement practices. It also goes beyond simply looking at the rate of adoption and asks what combination of total quality management and employee involvement programs has a positive impact. In addition, it presents important new findings on the growth and success of total quality management programs.

Because organizational effectiveness is such an important issue and interests such a broad audience, we wrote this book with a minimum of jargon and have avoided reporting the detailed results of our complex statistical analyses. Because our objective was to make this book readable by anyone interested in employee involvement and total quality management, we have presented the data in a manner that is accessible and easy to interpret. Managers, students, union leaders, employees, and anyone else interested in employee involvement and total quality management should find that the book offers valuable insights into what is happening in major companies.

Overview of the Contents. In Part One, we address the adoption rate of employee involvement practices. Specifically, we report on the use of information-sharing, knowledge-increasing, reward-system, and power-sharing practices. In each case, we compare their use in 1987, 1990, and 1993 and find a selective increase. Part One concludes with a section on patterns in the use of information, knowledge, reward, and power practices. The section provides a good sense of which practices appear together in organizations and of how different organizations are facing the challenge of balancing practices that affect information, knowledge, rewards, and power. It also provides interesting data on how widely different comprehensive approaches to employee involvement are adopted.

Part Two, focusing on total quality management programs and practices, finds widespread adoption of these. It also shows that total quality management programs and employee involvement programs are increasingly related and that typically employee involvement is part of total quality management.

In Part Three, we concentrate first on the results of employee involvement programs. We look at the success of those that focus primarily on reward systems. For example, we ask about the success of skill-based pay systems, gainsharing programs, and profit-sharing programs. The results are generally quite favorable. Next we examine the success of power-sharing programs, such as quality-circle programs, self-managing teams, and job enrichment; the results are also generally favorable. Part Three also reports the overall evaluation of employee involvement and total quality management activities in companies and considers their impact on both internal operating effectiveness and financial performance. The results are again quite favorable. Companies consistently find that employee involvement and total quality management practices have helped improve their internal operations and their financial results. There also is evidence that companies that have better financial performance are more likely to use employee involvement programs.

Part Four examines what type of organizations adopt employee involvement and total quality management. It compares large companies with small ones and service with manufacturing organizations. Consistent patterns emerge, showing that some types of organizations clearly are using employee involvement more than others. Part Four also considers unionization and the adoption of employee involvement. Finally, this part assesses the impact of the competitive environment on the adoption and success of employee involvement and total quality management practices, and reveals a clear relationship between them. The adoption of employee involvement and total quality management practices is usually a direct response to market pressures, particularly those that involve global competition.

Part Five explores the future of employee involvement and total quality management. First it considers the plans of organizations for adopting employee involvement and total quality management practices, as well as their expected spending rate. Next it looks at the types of changes that have occurred so far in the way the Fortune 1000 are managed, and it considers what the next changes are likely to be.

Acknowledgments. Our study is part of the research program of the Center for Effective Organizations. The center, which is part of the Graduate School of Business Administration at the University of Southern California, is sponsored by a number of corporations interested in supporting research on management. Their financial support helped make this study possible. The Sloan Foundation provided financial support that allowed us to do the financial analyses presented in the volume. The Association for Quality and Participation commissioned this study and provided support for the 1990 survey.

Founded in 1977, the Association for Quality and Participation (AQP) is a Cincinnati-based, not-for-profit professional association dedicated to promoting quality and participation in the workplace. AQP promotes these concepts through education courses, national and regional conferences, resource materials, publications (including *The Journal for Quality and Participation*), on-site training, a Professional Achievement Recognition System (PARS), and local chapters. With over 10,000 members and 84 chapters throughout North America, AQP continues to be at the forefront of the field, working to bring quality and participation to organizations of all types in an effort to help them create high performance, high-value workplaces.

A study like this requires that people in organizations take time to complete the questionnaires that we distributed. We are very appreciative of the time spent by members of the Fortune 1000 companies in responding to this survey.

Any research study of this magnitude requires a high level of staff support. We are fortunate at the Center for Effective Organizations to have a talented staff to assist our research activity. We would particularly like to acknowledge the excellent help we received in data collection and data analysis from Alice Yee Mark, Anna ter Veer, and Beth Neilson.

Los Angeles, California　　　　　　　　　　Edward E. Lawler III
April 1995　　　　　　　　　　　　　　Susan Albers Mohrman
　　　　　　　　　　　　　　　　　　Gerald E. Ledford, Jr.

The Authors

Edward E. Lawler III is professor of research at the University of Southern California (USC). He joined USC in 1978; in 1979 he founded and became director of the university's Center for Effective Organizations. Lawler received his B.A. degree (1960) from Brown University and his Ph.D. degree (1964) from the University of California, Berkeley, both in psychology. He has consulted with over one hundred organizations and four national governments on employee involvement, organizational change, and compensation. The author of over two hundred articles and twenty-two books, his works have been translated into seven languages. Lawler's most recent books include *Organizing for the Future: The New Logic for Managing Complex Organizations* (1993, with Jay R. Galbraith & Associates), *The Ultimate Advantage: Creating the High-Involvement Organization* (1992), *Strategic Pay: Aligning Organizational Strategies and Pay Systems* (1990), *Designing Performance Appraisal Systems: Aligning Appraisal and Organizational Realities* (1989, with A. M. Mohrman, Jr., and S. M. Resnick-West), and *High-Involvement Management: Participative Strategies for Improving Organizational Performance* (1986).

Susan Albers Mohrman is senior research scientist at the Center for Effective Organizations, Graduate School of Business Administration, University of Southern California. She received her A.B. degree (1967) from Stanford University in psychology and her Ph.D. degree (1978) from Northwestern University in organizational behavior. Mohrman has published papers and books on employee involvement, innovative approaches to the design of organizations, organizational development and change, high-technology organizations, union-management cooperative projects, team designs and lateral organizations, and innovative research and evaluation methodologies. She is an editor of *Large-Scale Organizational Change* (1989, with others), *Managing Complexity in High Technology Organizations* (1989), and *Doing Research That Is Useful for Theory and Practice* (1985, with others). Mohrman is coauthor of *Designing Team-Based Organizations: New Forms for Knowledge Work* (1995) and *Self-Designing Organizations: Learning How to Create High Performance* (1989).

Gerald E. Ledford, Jr., is senior research scientist at the Center for Effective Organizations, Graduate School of Business Administration,

University of Southern California. He received his B.A. degree (1973) from George Washington University in psychology and his M.A. (1979) and Ph.D. (1984) from the University of Michigan, also in psychology. He has conducted research, published, and consulted on a wide variety of approaches to improving organizational effectiveness and employee well-being, including employee involvement, innovative reward systems, organization design, job design, and union-management cooperation. He has done especially extensive research on high-involvement organizations and innovative reward systems. Ledford has published fifty articles and book chapters and is coauthor or coeditor of four books, including *Employee Involvement and Total Quality Management: Practices and Results in Fortune 1000 Companies (1992), Large-Scale Organizational Change (1989),* and *Employee Involvement in America: A Study of Contemporary Practice* (1989, with E. E. Lawler III and S. A. Mohrman). He is cowinner of the Yoder-Heneman Personnel Research Award (1990) from the Society for Human Resource Management and was named an Ascendant Scholar (1991) by the Western Academy of Management.

Introduction: Studying Employee Involvement and Total Quality Management

Employee involvement, participative management, democratic management, and *total quality management* are familiar terms to most managers. They have been discussed by some and advocated by others for several decades now. The terms gained increased prominence in the 1980s because of the new economic realities that faced business. To succeed, many American companies had to increase their performance significantly (Grayson and O'Dell, 1988; Dertouzos, Lester, and Solow, 1989; Levine, 1995). The most intriguing suggestion about how to improve performance was that organizations change their organization and management systems to be more participative by involving employees in problem solving, decision making, and the financial success of the business. This idea is an important part of all total quality management programs, and it is a major part of such employee involvement practices as gainsharing and work teams.

The involvement approach is based on the idea that organizations should be designed from top to bottom so that employees are in control of their destiny and able to participate in the business of the organization. In order to participate in the business, employees at all levels need power, information, knowledge, and rewards that are relevant to business performance (Lawler, 1986). Thus, in our studies of employee involvement we ask questions about how business information, training and knowledge, power, and rewards (particularly rewards for performance) are spread throughout the organization. Of particular interest is the extent to which employees producing the products or offering the services have a sense of controlling their work, receiving information about performance, and being rewarded for the performance of their organization.

Of course, true involvement takes more than just spreading any one, two, or three of the four key features—power, information, knowledge, and rewards—to all levels of the organization (Lawler, 1986; 1992). All four of these features must exist at all levels of the organization. Only when this is the case can the individuals performing the work actually see a relationship between their efforts and the success or failure of the organization. In looking at the employee involvement practices of organizations, it is therefore important to study the degree to which all of these features (information, knowledge, power, and rewards) are pushed downward.

Total quality management programs place a strong emphasis on employee involvement in addition to calling for a series of specific practices that are aimed at improving quality. Particularly with respect to their use of teams and the open sharing of performance data, there is substantial overlap with most employee involvement efforts. Thus, although it can be looked at separately, total quality management is closely related to employee involvement and needs to be studied as a related, and in some cases as an integrated, effort.

The 1990s have seen an increased focus on the use of organization and management practices to gain competitive advantage. Indeed it has been argued that in many situations they are the best long-term source of competitive advantage (Lawler, 1992; Pfeffer, 1994). The challenge is to identify organization designs and management practices that create capabilities leading to higher levels of performance than those obtained by competitors. The current interest in organizational learning and process reengineering is clear testimony to the search of many companies for improved organizational capabilities. Not surprisingly most approaches to both organizational learning and reengineering place an emphasis on employee involvement as the best approach to creating high performance work organizations.

Any assessment of corporate practices in the areas of employee involvement and total quality management needs to look at the adoption rate for programs and practices that are consistent with them. In 1987, we conducted a study of the Fortune 1000 firms in order to determine whether companies had incorporated employee involvement practices into their approach to management (Lawler, Ledford, and Mohrman, 1989). In 1990, we repeated this study and added a series of questions on total quality management (Lawler, Mohrman, and Ledford, 1992). The 1990 study, while showing an increase in employee involvement activities, still indicated that a very low percentage of the employees in the largest U.S. corporations work in an environment that could be described as high involvement or high performance. Companies generally reported that they were very satisfied with the results of their employee involvement activities and that they planned to expand them.

The data from our 1987 and 1990 studies suggested that the vast majority of the firms that use employee involvement do so to improve the bottom line of the organization. Companies are particularly interested in gains in productivity, quality, and employee motivation. Close behind is the desire to increase employee morale. Trailing far behind are value and ethical reasons. In short, companies seem to feel that it is good business to practice employee involvement. This finding undoubtedly helps to explain why, even though the idea of employee involvement has been around for decades, it has received significant attention only in the last ten to twenty years. Simply stated, in this period organizations have felt serious competitive pressures and have therefore been willing to consider management-style changes.

Purpose of Study. This study examines the degree to which companies are using management practices, policies, and behaviors that are supportive of employee involvement and total quality management. It especially assesses how much change has occurred from 1987 to 1993. In addition, the study focuses on the results of employee involvement and total quality management, the degree of compatibility between them, and the environments that organizations face. It also identifies organizational policies and practices that are supportive of employee involvement and the obstacles to that involvement. Finally, it reviews how total quality management practices are related to employee involvement programs.

Study Method. The 1987 survey was conducted by the U.S. General Accounting Office (GAO). Michael Dulworth was the GAO project leader. At the inception of the study, the GAO brought together a consultants' panel to advise it on the study's design. This panel included experts on employee involvement systems from both the federal and the private sectors. A design team, including representatives from the University of Southern California's Center for Effective Organizations (Lawler, Mohrman, and Ledford) and Michael Dulworth from GAO, developed the employee involvement survey questionnaire.

The 1990 survey was conducted by the Center for Effective Organizations at the University of Southern California; financial support was provided by the Association for Quality and Participation. It used many of the same questions that were asked in the 1987 study. In addition, it asked a series of questions about total quality management programs and practices. The questions were added because of growing interest in these programs and their close relationship to employee involvement.

The 1993 survey is a further refinement of the 1990 survey. The most significant change concerns total quality management. Additional questions were added because of both the increased interest in these programs and the continued focus on quality as a source of competitive advantage. A few new questions were also added with respect to employee involvement programs; these were intended to improve our understanding of organizational patterns concerning the use of employee involvement and their impact. Resource A contains a copy of the 1993 questionnaire. A glossary defining the employee involvement terms accompanied all surveys. The glossary from the 1993 questionnaire can be found in Resource B.

Study Sample. The 1987 survey was sent by the GAO to 934 of the companies listed in the 1986 Fortune 1000 listing of the 500 largest service companies and the 500 largest industrial firms. The actual number of companies surveyed was fewer than 1,000 because of acquisitions and mergers. Responses numbered 476, a 51 percent response rate. The responding organizations employed almost nine million full-time employees.

The 1990 survey was sent to 987 organizations on the 1989 Fortune 1000 list by the Center for Effective Organizations at the University of Southern California. Responses were received from 313 organizations, a response rate of 32 percent. One hundred companies responded to both the 1987 survey and the 1990 survey. The 1993 survey was sent to 985 companies from the Fortune 1992 listing of the 1,000 largest manufacturing and service companies. Responses were received from 279 companies, a response rate of 28 percent. One hundred and thirty companies responded to both the 1990 and the 1993 questionnaires.

Our 1990 and 1993 surveys used many of the same mailing and follow-up procedures employed by the GAO in 1987 but did not obtain as high a response rate. The higher response rate to the 1987 survey was most likely due to its sponsorship by the GAO, a credible government agency. Nevertheless, response rates of 32 and 28 percent are impressive given the large number of surveys being sent to companies today and the length (eighteen pages) of the surveys. They are large enough return rates to allow some important comparisons among the three surveys. They are also sufficiently large to permit some interesting comparisons among the different types of companies that are represented in the 1993 sample.

Although all three were sent to companies listed in the Fortune 1000 at the time of each study, the surveys were not sent to the same companies. The period from 1987 to 1993 saw significant shifts in the makeup of the Fortune 1000; only 650 companies were on both the 1986 and 1992 Fortune 1000 lists. This rate of change in the Fortune 1000 helps account for the fact that we often did not receive responses from the same companies when we did our surveys in 1987, 1990, and 1993.

A broad array of service and industrial firms is represented in the samples. Approximately half of the 1987, 1990, and the 1993 samples come from the service sector and approximately half from the manufacturing sector. The median size of the organizations in the samples was 9,200 employees in 1987, 10,000 in 1990, and 11,000 in 1993. The mean distribution of types of employees in these organizations was almost identical, as the following indicates:

	1987	1990	1993
Hourly/Clerical	59%	59%	54%
Technical/Professional	20%	20%	24%
Supervisory/Managerial	14%	14%	15%
Other	8%	9%	6%

Our conclusion is that the samples appear to be generally comparable even though the response rate is somewhat lower for the 1990 and 1993 surveys. This is an important point because it means that any differences in results among the surveys are likely to be due to actual changes in how the Fortune 1000 companies are managing rather than being a product of different companies responding to the three surveys. Where possible, we checked this conclusion by comparing the 1987, 1990, and 1993 survey data for those companies that responded to more than one survey, and we found the results to be generally consistent.

In 35 percent of the cases, responses to the 1993 survey came from managers responsible for human resources, employee involvement, or total quality. The other 65 percent were completed by a wide variety of senior executives, typically someone in the corporate office two levels below the chief executive officer.

Our data do have important limitations. They address only the 1,000 largest companies in the United States and thus say nothing about what is happening in the vast numbers of smaller companies that constitute a large and growing part of the U.S. economy. Furthermore, they represent a view from the top. Senior managers completed most of the surveys. The views from other levels in the organization—from middle managers, front-line supervisors, production workers, and union leaders—may be different.

Despite its limitations, this report is the most comprehensive accounting of practices and approaches to employee involvement and total quality management currently available. No comparable data set exists covering employee involvement and total quality management activities in such a broad array of corporations. Particularly important is the possibility of comparing 1987, 1990, and 1993 data in order to determine changing patterns of adoption and impact. This comparison offers a unique opportunity to investigate employee involvement and total quality efforts at various stages of implementation and in a variety of industrial and service organizations. From these data, we are confident that we can produce research findings useful to all companies trying to engage more fully the energies and talents of their people in addressing the competitive challenges that lie ahead.

PART ONE

Adoption of Employee Involvement Practices

SECTION 1
Sharing Information

Basic to employee involvement in companies is the sharing of information about business performance, plans, and goals. Without that information, it is difficult for individuals to understand how the business is doing and to make meaningful contributions to its success. In addition, participation in planning and setting direction is impossible without business information. In many cases, it is also impossible for employees to make good suggestions about how products and services can be improved and about how work processes in their area can be done more effectively. Finally, it is also difficult for employees to alter their behavior in response to changing conditions and get feedback about the effectiveness of their performance and that of the organization. In the absence of business information, individuals are usually limited simply to carrying out prescribed tasks and roles in a relatively automatic bureaucratic way. They are prevented from understanding, participating in, and managing the overall business direction and results.

Figure 1.1 provides responses to a question on the types of information that are shared. As it shows, most organizations share information about the company's overall operating results with 60 or more percent of their employees. This was true in 1987 and 1990, and it is again true in 1993. We anticipated this finding, since every organization in the study is a public corporation and by law must provide financial information to shareholders. At a minimum, it would seem that organizations would give their employees the same information that they give their shareholders in their annual reports.

If anything is surprising about the results shown in Figure 1.1, it is how many organizations do not share financial results with all employees. The evidence does show a small increase in the number of companies sharing financial information. However, 17 percent of the companies still do not give information about their performance to most of their employees even when it is public. Not shown in Figure 1.1 is the further finding that only 45 percent of the companies provide all their employees information about overall operating results. The obvious conclusion here seems to be that in a significant number of companies some employees are not treated as important stakeholders in and contributors to the company's performance.

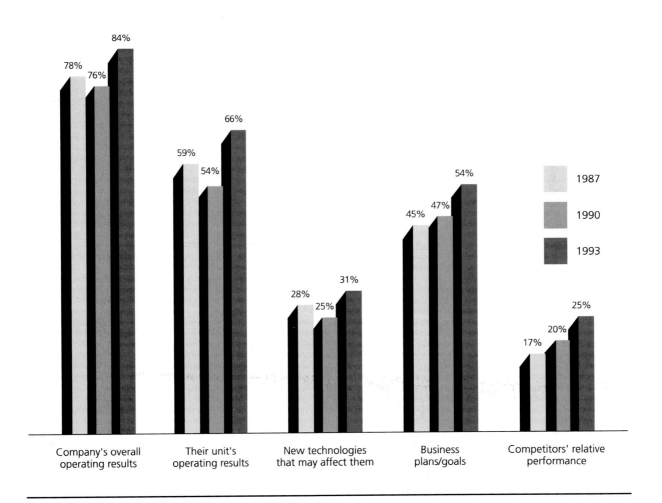

Figure 1.1. Percentage Indicating More Than 60 Percent of Employees Were Given Information.

Although important in helping employees view the business as a whole, information about the general performance of a large company may be of limited utility to many employees. The corporate operating results are a considerable distance from many job activities and may not relate very directly to what some employees do. Information on their *unit's* operating results is likely to be much more meaningful to employees.

As can be seen from Figure 1.1, 66 percent of the companies do share data on the performance of their work unit with more than 60 percent of their employees. But more than a third of these companies do not regularly share unit operating results with most employees. Only a little over half (54 percent) of companies provide regular information on the plans and goals of the business. In addition, it is clear from the data in Figure 1.1 that the typical employee gets extremely limited feedback on relative business performance. Only 25 percent of the organizations provide data on competitors' performance to most or all employees.

The situation is similar with respect to information sharing about new technologies. Only 31 percent of the corporations say that they provide most of their employees with information about new technologies that may affect them. Without this information, it is impossible for employees to participate in the planning activities that are involved in the start-up of new technologies or to influence decisions about their adoption and acquisition. Lack of information also prevents employees from preparing personally for technological transitions.

There has been a general trend over time toward distributing more information to employees. The increases from 1987 to 1993 are not large, but they are in the direction of greater information sharing. This trend fits with the increased interest in benchmarking as well as the increasing competitive pressures faced by businesses.

As a general rule, the more business unit-specific the information, the less likely that most employees are provided with it. This is understandable in one respect: in many cases, nothing requires organizations to distribute information about how a business unit is doing. However, not supplying this information to employees may have significant costs and certainly is a major obstacle to employee involvement. The typical employee in companies that do not share information may not understand how well the business is doing and is likely to have little sense of what it must do to be competitive. Awareness of corporate results is helpful in understanding the larger context, but it is at the unit level where most employees can make a difference and can relate to performance results. Information at this level is also what they need in order to contribute ideas and suggestions and be involved in the business.

To get an idea of the concentration of these information-sharing approaches within companies, we counted the number of different kinds of information given to at least 40 percent of employees. Table 1.1 illustrates the percentage of companies sharing from none to all of the five kinds of information listed in Figure 1.1. Again, the data from 1987, 1990, and 1993 are very similar. The 1993 data show that 49 percent of companies share four or more of the kinds of information with at least 40 percent of employees; 25 percent share all kinds. This finding, which suggests that more companies may be

Table 1.1	Percentage of Companies Sharing Information with More Than 40 Percent of Employees.		
NUMBER OF KINDS OF INFORMATION SHARED	1987 (N=323)	1990 (N=313)	1993 (N=279)
0	6	8	6
1	11	15	11
2	19	21	14
3	22	17	20
4	26	23	24
5	16	16	25

Five possible kinds: company's overall operating results, unit operating results, advance information on new technology, business plans/goals, competitors' relative performance.

broadly providing information than was true in 1990, is important since sharing all or most of this information may be a necessary precondition for high levels of employee involvement.

Do employee involvement programs increase the information flow in organizations? As shown in Figure 1.2, the answer appears to be yes. The most common response to this question in 1987, 1990, and 1993—that involvement activities increase information flow to a moderate degree—was to be expected, since information is so critical to all aspects of involvement. If anything is unexpected, it is that the responses to this question were not more positive.

Our results show that Fortune 1000 corporations share only limited information with employees. There is some sign of change from 1987 to 1993 but not the amount that might be expected given the critical role of information in many involvement and total quality programs. In essence, many organizations provide only what the law requires them to make available to shareholders: overall business results. Most employees do not get good information on the direction and success of the business. Given this fact, it is hard to imagine most employees being meaningfully involved in decisions affecting anything more than their immediate job duties.

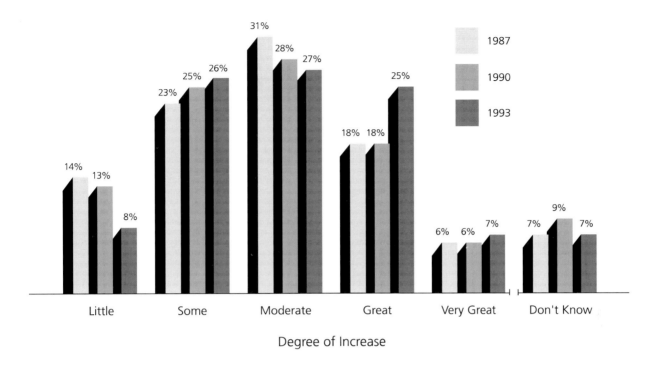

Figure 1.2. Percentage Indicating Degree to Which Information Has Increased as a Result of Employee Involvement.

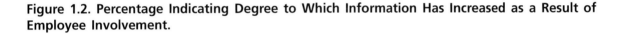

SECTION 2

Developing Knowledge

Much of the writing on national competitiveness during the 1980s and early 1990s has stressed the importance of skill development (for example, see Porter, 1990; Reich, 1991). Similar conclusions have been reached by studies that have focused on the condition of schools in the United States (Secretary's Commission on Achieving Necessary Skills, 1991). Without the right skills, it is unwise for individuals to participate in a business and to influence its direction. At a more basic level, without skills, individuals cannot do many jobs effectively and also cannot get good jobs.

Table 2.1 reports on the prevalence of training for the types of skills frequently identified as being necessary for effective employee involvement and total quality management (Commission on the Skills of the American Workforce, 1990). Three of these skills are essentially interpersonal and group skills. These are included because so many employee involvement and total quality processes involve meetings, interpersonal interactions, group problem solving,

Table 2.1	Percentage Indicating That More Than 60 Percent of Employees Had Training in Past Three Years.		
TYPES OF TRAINING	1987 (N=323)	1990 (N=313)	1993 (N=279)
Group Decision-Making/ Problem-Solving Skills	5	6	16
Leadership Skills	4	3	8
Skills in Understanding the Business (e.g., accounting, finance, etc.)	4	2	5
Quality/Statistical Analysis Skills	6	9	22
Team-Building Skills	5	8	17
Job-Skills Training	N/A	35	48
Cross-Training	N/A	N/A	13

and influencing others. The two technical skills, quality/statistical analysis and business understanding, are included because they are central to the content of organizational improvement and total quality management efforts. Finally, we asked about job-skills training (1990 and 1993 only) and about cross-training (1993 only).

As can be seen from the table, during the last three years, most employees were not trained in either interpersonal skills or the kind of technical/analytical skills necessary for an employee involvement or total quality program to work effectively (Deming, 1986; Juran, 1989). However, the results are different from those that were obtained in 1987 and 1990. Perhaps because of the national focus on total quality management and statistical analysis, there is a definite increase in the training of employees in quality skills and in group decision making.

The situation is much the same with respect to interpersonal skills. Although there is an encouraging increase in team-building skills, most individuals simply are not trained in the various interpersonal skills needed for them to participate in problem-solving groups and team-based decision making.

The data are more positive with respect to job skills; 48 percent of the companies surveyed provided training to most of their employees, a significant increase from 1990 (35 percent). Further, 13 percent cross-trained a majority of their employees. Although the trend with respect to training is encouraging, these levels stand in notable contrast to the policies of such exemplary companies as Motorola, which mandate one week's training for all employees each year (see Wiggenhorn, 1990).

Despite the importance of employees' understanding the business, only 5 percent of organizations have recently trained more than 60 percent of their employees in understanding financial reports and business results. This number is little changed from 1987 and 1990. Given this lack of training, it is unreasonable to expect employees to understand business performance and to be able to contribute to it in an informed, self-directed way.

What accounts for the poor, if improving, record of most corporations in the area of training? One possibility is that the window is too small. We asked about training only in the prior three years; it may be that many organizations trained their employees earlier. Unfortunately there is no way of knowing whether this is true, but it seems unlikely given the results of our 1987 and 1990 survey. Data from a variety of international comparative studies also suggest that U.S. manufacturing companies are relatively low spenders on training (see, for example, Kochan and Osterman, 1994; Pfeffer, 1994).

It may be that setting 60 percent of employees trained as the threshold represents too high a level for many companies to reach. Table 2.2 uses a lower threshold of 20 percent. This picture is somewhat more positive. The 1993 data suggest that organizations have significantly increased their training in several areas. Particularly significant is the increase in training associated with teams and quality improvement processes. The 88 percent number for job training is encouraging. However, a note of caution is in order here. This result may represent nothing more than a commitment to traditional on-the-job training. Business understanding skills clearly stands out as the area where the least training is done.

A count of how many types of training are being done by each company is shown in Table 2.3. It shows that during the three years before these data were collected, only 3 percent of the responding companies trained 40 percent or more of their employees in these five areas. Forty-four percent did not train 40 percent or more in any of the areas, a significant decrease from 1990 to 1993.

Table 2.2	Percentage Indicating That More Than 20 Percent of Employees Had Training in Past Three Years.		

TYPES OF TRAINING	1987 (N=323)	1990 (N=313)	1993 (N=279)
Group Decision-Making/ Problem-Solving Skills	57	55	72
Leadership Skills	63	54	67
Skills in Understanding the Business (e.g., accounting, finance, etc.)	50	39	42
Quality/Statistical Analysis Skills	42	43	63
Team-Building Skills	52	56	75
Job-Skills Training	N/A	84	88
Cross-Training	N/A	N/A	69

Table 2.3	Percentage of Companies Providing Five Kinds of Training to More Than 40 Percent of Employees in Past Three Years.		

NUMBER OF KINDS OF TRAINING PROVIDED	1987 (N=323)	1990 (N=313)	1993 (N=279)
0	63	59	44
1	16	22	15
2	12	8	19
3	6	7	11
4	2	2	7
5	1	1	3

Five possible kinds: group decision making/problem solving, leadership, business understanding (accounting, etc.), quality/statistical analysis, team building.

The results change significantly when job skills are included as a kind of training (as is shown in Table 2.4). With them included, only 20 percent of the companies provided no training in these areas to 40 percent or more of their employees. This represents a significant change from the 1990 results and indicates that more training is being done.

Do employee involvement programs lead to more training and skill development? The data in Figure 2.1 suggest that they do. Most companies indicate that involvement has led to some or to a moderate increase in skill development.

Overall, the data on training suggest an improving situation with respect to the training of workers in U.S. corporations. Most major U.S. corporations apparently are making greater investments in training. This is good news given the many studies that show that the American workforce is often poorly prepared to perform the work in those businesses facing global competition (Dertouzos, Lester, and Solow, 1989; Reich, 1991). Although training is growing, it still appears to fall short of the level needed if employee involvement and

Table 2.4	Percentage of Companies Providing Six Kinds of Training to More Than 40 Percent of Employees in Past Three Years.	
NUMBER OF KINDS OF TRAINING PROVIDED	1990 (N=313)	1993 (N=279)
0	34	20
1	32	28
2	19	14
3	6	19
4	6	10
5	2	6
6	1	3

Six possible kinds: group decision making/problem solving, leadership, business understanding (accounting, etc.), quality/statistical analysis, team building, job-skills training.

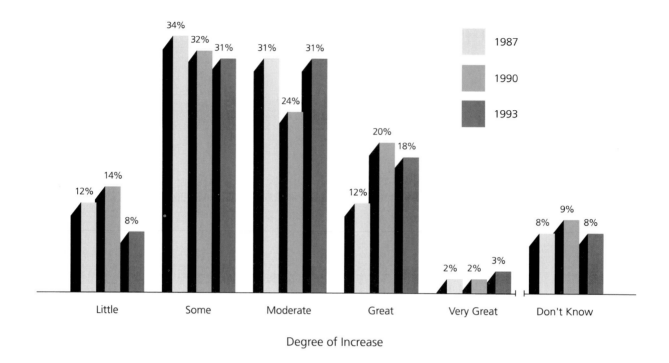

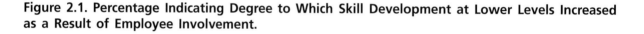

Figure 2.1. Percentage Indicating Degree to Which Skill Development at Lower Levels Increased as a Result of Employee Involvement.

total quality management are to work—indeed, for most businesses to perform effectively, regardless of what management approach they use. This situation is particularly true with respect to the skills necessary for employees to become full business partners.

SECTION 3

Rewarding Performance

Basing rewards on organizational performance is one way to ensure that employees are involved in and care about the performance of their company (Lawler, 1990). It also helps ensure that they share in the gains that result from any performance improvement. Table 3.1 shows the popularity of five approaches to paying for performance.

Individual incentive plans are usually not very supportive of employee involvement or total quality management. They focus on individuals' performance and do not tie the individual into the overall success of the business; moreover, they can interfere with team-

		None (0%)	Almost None (1–20%)	Some (21–40%)	About Half (41–60%)	Most (61–80%)	Almost All (81–99%)	All (100%)
Individual Incentives	1987	13	49	27	6	2	1	2
	1990	10	46	24	8	5	3	5
	1993	10	40	30	8	3	4	5
Work-Group or Team Incentives	1987			— — not asked — —				
	1990	41	38	10	6	1	2	3
	1993	30	40	14	6	3	3	5
Profit Sharing	1987	35	20	11	4	5	10	15
	1990	37	19	7	4	6	10	17
	1993	34	23	7	4	3	11	19
Gainsharing	1987	74	19	4	1	0	1	1
	1990	61	28	8	1	1	1	0
	1993	58	26	7	2	3	2	2
Employee Stock Ownership Plan	1987	39	8	4	4	6	10	28
	1990	36	9	6	3	5	13	29
	1993	29	9	9	4	6	14	30
Stock Option Plan	1993	15	56	15	2	1	2	10
Nonmonetary Recognition Awards for Performance	1990	9	23	18	10	13	10	17
	1993	6	22	17	7	10	17	22

Table 3.1 — Percentage of Employees Covered by Performance-Based Reward Practices.

work and problem solving. The pattern for individual incentives shown in Table 3.1 reveals that all but 10 percent of the corporations report having some employees covered by individual incentives; however, these systems usually cover less than 21 percent of the workforce. A comparison among 1987, 1990, and 1993 shows no significant change in the use of individual incentive plans.

Team incentives can be supportive of employee involvement activities such as work teams and problem-solving groups. They are increasingly popular. Seventy percent of all companies use them, although when used they tend to cover small numbers of employees (fewer than 20 percent). This finding makes sense: many individuals do not work in teams; thus, using team incentives for them is not appropriate.

Profit sharing, stock ownership, stock options, and gainsharing are approaches that can link employees more closely to the success of the business and reward them for it. These systems are often cited as the reward approaches that are most supportive of employee involvement (Lawler, 1990; Blinder, 1990). The results show that profit sharing and employee stock ownership are the most widely used and the most likely to be available to most or all employees.

Particularly interesting is the fact that stock ownership plans are available to all employees in 30 percent of the corporations surveyed, though there is little evidence of an increase in their popularity from 1987 to 1993. It is likely that this result reflects the widespread use of stock purchase plans (Blasi, 1988; Rosen, Klein, and Young, 1986). In 29 percent of the corporations surveyed, stock ownership plans are not available to any employees. It is one of the few practices that companies tend to offer to all or none of their employees.

Only 19 percent of the companies cover all employees with profit sharing, and only 66 percent cover any of their employees with a profit-sharing plan. Many profit-sharing plans defer payments until retirement (Lawler, 1990). Thus it seems safe to conclude that profit sharing is not acting as an important motivator of involvement or performance in most companies. A comparison between the 1990 and 1993 results shows no significant increase in the use of profit sharing despite an increasing emphasis in the management literature on the use of variable or bonus-based pay (Blinder, 1990; Schuster and Zingheim, 1992).

Historically, gainsharing has been most closely identified with employee involvement since it stresses involvement as key to the success of its financial bonus system. As shown in Table 3.1, gainsharing is clearly the least popular approach. Fifty-eight percent of responding companies say none of their employees are covered by a gainsharing plan. Of the corporations that have gainsharing plans, virtually all offer it to a minority of their total workforce. Rare (only 2 percent of companies that responded in 1993) is the corporation that covers all employees with gainsharing.

A comparison between the 1987 and 1990 results shows a significant increase in the use of gainsharing; however, a comparison between the 1990 and the 1993 data does not show an increase. One possible explanation is that gainsharing plans have reached the point where they have been installed in a significant percentage of the situations where they fit well. As a result, further growth will be slow and may depend on the development of new approaches to gainsharing that allow these plans to be installed in new settings.

The actual amount of employee involvement–oriented reward activity may be a bit inflated in Table 3.1 because profit-sharing and employee stock ownership plans (ESOPs) are included. Many profit-sharing plans have been around for years and are often best thought of as fringe benefits rather than incentives. Many ESOPs have been installed for tax advantages and are not tied to employee involvement (Blasi, 1988). In addition, the effectiveness of profit-sharing plans and ESOPs can be questioned for two reasons. First, the "line of sight" for profit sharing and ESOPs is often quite poor; individual employees may not know how to affect such distant, aggregate measures as profit or stock price. Second, the general lack of information and knowledge about the business that exists in many companies limits the line of sight even more. Without information and knowledge, variable rewards often appear arbitrary and capricious, rather than motivating and involving.

Nonmonetary recognition programs are sometimes used to support employee involvement efforts. They are also frequently advocated by the proponents of total quality management programs. Table 3.1 shows that most organizations have recognition programs, but they cover all employees in only 22 percent of the companies. This suggests that they typically are targeted at special activities and groups. The data do show a little growth in their popularity from 1990 to 1993; this may well reflect their increasingly being used as part of total quality management programs.

Figure 3.1 suggests that the responding companies feel employee involvement has had a limited effect on the degree to which

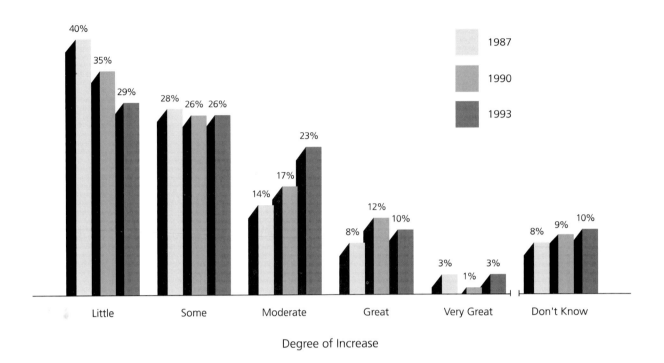

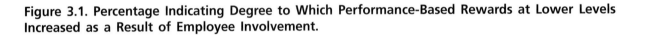

Figure 3.1. Percentage Indicating Degree to Which Performance-Based Rewards at Lower Levels Increased as a Result of Employee Involvement.

performance-based rewards have increased at lower levels. In fact, according to our respondents, rewards have been affected less by employee involvement than have information sharing and knowledge. The 1993, 1990, and the 1987 data show similar results.

Table 3.2 shows the concentration of the five pay-for-performance reward-system approaches. Twenty-four percent of companies are using none of them widely, and only 14 percent use three or more widely. The results clearly establish that most organizations do not make a significant effort to reward most individuals for their performance. The opportunity therefore exists for most organizations to reward many more individuals for performance and, as a result, to increase their level of involvement in their organizations.

Table 3.3 presents the results for a number of additional reward-system practices considered to be supportive of employee involvement. The first of these practices, all-salaried pay, reduces the distinctions between the exempt and nonexempt classifications of employees, thus creating a situation where the pay system is

Table 3.2	Percentage of Companies Using Performance-Based Reward Practices with More Than 40 Percent of Employees.	
NUMBER OF KINDS OF REWARD PRACTICES	1990 (N=313)	1993 (N=279)
0	29	24
1	38	41
2	24	21
3	8	8
4	2	5
5	0	1

Five possible kinds: individual incentives, profit sharing, gainsharing, employee stock ownership, work-group or team incentives.

congruent with the notion of an egalitarian workforce. Table 3.3 shows that over two-thirds of companies use this approach to some extent. A comparison between 1990 and 1993 shows no significant increase in the use of all-salaried workforces.

When pay is based on knowledge and skill, it rewards individuals for their capability and flexibility to contribute to the organization. As a person learns more and can contribute more to the organization, pay is increased (Ledford, 1991). This approach fosters and rewards cross-training and makes possible the flexible deployment of people. It also can be supportive of teaming and encouraging individuals to learn skills needed for them to be involved in the business. Finally, it promotes a broader understanding of how the business operates, a skill that can be useful in addressing complex problems. Table 3.3 shows that 60 percent of companies use this approach to some extent, although most with only a minority (1 to 20 percent) of the workforce.

A comparison among the 1987, 1990, and 1993 data shows significant growth in the use of skill-based pay. The number of

Table 3.3

Percentage of Employees Covered by EI-Supportive Reward Practices.

		None (0%)	Almost None (1–20%)	Some (21–40%)	About Half (41–60%)	Most (61–80%)	Almost All (81–99%)	All (100%)
All-Salaried Pay Systems	1987	29	15	13	10	12	11	10
	1990	36	18	14	10	7	9	7
	1993	27	18	11	13	11	11	9
Knowledge/ Skill-Based Pay	1987	60	25	7	2	2	2	2
	1990	49	34	11	2	1	1	1
	1993	40	37	12	4	2	2	3
Flexible, Cafeteria-Style Benefits	1987	66	7	4	3	2	6	13
	1990	46	12	5	4	5	9	20
	1993	32	9	7	4	7	12	30
Employment Security	1987	47	14	6	2	6	8	18
	1990	47	20	6	4	6	9	8
	1993	63	13	5	2	3	5	9
Open Pay Information	1993	34	17	8	7	6	9	20

companies employing it increased from 40 percent to 51 percent to 60 percent. In several respects, this is an important change. Skill-based pay is not an "extra." It represents a major change in the way an organization determines pay. Many pay systems have been in place for decades and are not easily altered; they must be changed in a major way if skill-based pay is adopted. Therefore it is particularly impressive that a significant increase has occurred in the use of skill-based pay.

Flexible benefits programs provide employees with some control over how the benefit portion of their compensation package is distributed. This approach fits with the employee involvement philosophy of moving the responsibility for decisions to those individuals who are affected by them. Sixty-eight percent of companies use flexible benefits.

Flexible benefits, which increased tremendously in their popularity from 1987 to 1993, show the biggest growth of any pay practice studied. Although flexible benefits programs fit with employee involvement because of their emphasis on employee choice in the reward mix, the increased adoption of this approach may have more to do with controlling benefit costs and meeting the needs of an increasingly diverse workforce than with supporting involvement. The cost of benefits, particularly health care, has been increasing dramatically, and many companies are using flexible benefits and cost sharing as ways to control their costs (Lawler, 1990).

The results concerning employment security are interesting. It has been argued that security of employment is an important enabler of involvement and total quality management (see, for example, Pfeffer, 1994). Without job security, employees may fear that any improvement they make will threaten their jobs and those of others. As a result, individuals may feel hesitant to get involved in improvement activities. The results show a significant decline in the number of companies with employment security. Most noticeable is the increase from 47 percent to 63 percent of companies covering no employees with job security. Somewhat surprising, given the present business conditions, is the finding that 9 percent of these Fortune 1000 companies still cover all employees.

Open pay information is one way to assure that employees understand how they are paid, a necessary precondition to their participation in decisions about their pay and that of other employees. The results show an interesting split among companies: 20 percent supply all employees with open information while 34 percent give none. Clearly these companies are operating with two quite different philosophies with respect to providing information about pay.

Overall the data suggest that organizations are continuing to change their reward-system practices. Organizations are slowly increasing their use of skill-based pay and certain pay-for-performance approaches. Moving performance-based rewards throughout an organization and adding skill-based pay are difficult but potentially critical to the success of employee involvement. Failure to take these steps may limit the effectiveness of involvement; without them, employees are likely to see themselves as having little direct stake in organizational performance and may not feel rewarded for adding to their skills.

SECTION 4

Redistributing Power

Moving power downward in organizations often requires structural changes. In order to get some sense of how active organizations are in moving decision making to lower levels, the survey asked about the existence of a number of specific structural approaches. These approaches can be divided into two basic types.

The first type involves special meetings or problem-solving activities that are separate from the normal day-to-day work processes. These are often referred to as parallel organizational structures (Lawler and Mohrman, 1985; Lawler, 1992). The best known activity of this type is the quality circle. Although problem-solving activities do move some power downward, they are very limited in their impact (Ledford, Lawler, and Mohrman, 1988). Typically employees only provide input and recommendations; they do not make substantial decisions, nor do they have the budget or power to implement decisions.

As can be seen in Table 4.1, the majority of organizations report using some form of parallel structure, and many use more than one. Quality circles are used in 65 percent of all companies, virtually the same percentage as in 1990. Other types of participation groups are used by 91 percent of all companies. The use of parallel structures is generally limited to fewer than half of the employees in the organization, a situation that necessarily limits their impact.

A comparison of the 1990 with the 1993 data shows an increase in the use of participation groups. This increase is significant and somewhat surprising given the lack of change in the use of quality circles. Apparently companies are adopting participation groups instead of expanding their use of quality circles.

Union-management quality of work life committees have been tried in a much smaller percentage of the companies. This finding, of course, follows from the relatively low level of union membership in the United States and in these companies (fewer than 50 percent have union members). Although a comparison between 1987 and 1990 shows a 10 percent increase in the percentage of companies using this approach, a comparison between 1990 and 1993 shows no significant change.

Table 4.1 **Percentage of Employees Covered by Parallel Power-Sharing Practices.**

		None (0%)	Almost None (1–20%)	Some (21–40%)	About Half (41–60%)	Most (61–80%)	Almost All (81–99%)	All (100%)
Quality Circles	1987	39	32	18	7	2	0	1
	1990	34	36	19	7	4	1	1
	1993	35	32	19	6	5	3	1
Employee Participation Groups Other Than QCs	1987	30	33	21	9	3	2	1
	1990	14	35	30	11	5	3	3
	1993	9	26	31	14	13	5	3
Union-Management QWL Committees	1987	70	20	7	2	1	1	0
	1990	65	23	9	2	0	0	1
	1993	65	22	6	3	2	2	1
Survey Feedback	1987	32	22	17	6	7	6	10
	1990	23	26	20	5	4	7	16
	1993	15	19	15	8	9	10	25
Suggestion System	1987	17	17	16	7	11	11	21
	1990	14	24	14	7	10	12	19
	1993	15	26	19	11	7	9	14

Survey feedback is an activity that does not necessarily entail the establishment of a parallel structure since it often takes place in established work groups. However, it is often seen as an "extra" or special activity. As can be seen in Table 4.1, 85 percent of companies use it for at least some employees. Survey feedback shows a significant increase in popularity from 1987 to 1990 and from 1990 to 1993.

The 1993 survey also asked about the use of suggestion systems. Eighty-five percent of the companies report using them, although only a small percentage cover most of their employees with them. Although they are one of the oldest and perhaps least powerful approaches, suggestion systems continue to be popular and show no sign of becoming less so.

Table 4.2 provides the results of programs that are part of the work-redesign approach to moving power downward. Job enrichment, self-managed work teams, and minibusiness units involve a substantial change in the basic structure of the organization and are aimed at moving important decisions into the hands of individuals and teams performing the basic manufacturing or service work of the company.

Table 4.2		Percentage of Employees Covered by Work-Redesign Practices.						
		None (0%)	Almost None (1–20%)	Some (21–40%)	About Half (41–60%)	Most (61–80%)	Almost All (81–99%)	All (100%)
Job Enrichment or Redesign	1987	40	38	12	6	2	2	1
	1990	25	43	23	6	2	0	1
	1993	18	40	25	8	4	3	3
Self-Managing Work Teams	1987	72	20	6	1	0	0	0
	1990	53	37	9	1	0	0	0
	1993	32	49	15	3	2	0	0
Minibusiness Units	1987	75	18	4	1	1	0	0
	1990	72	23	3	1	0	1	0
	1993	56	23	14	3	4	1	0
Employee Committees Concerned with Policy and/or Strategy	1993	35	45	13	5	2	1	0

As shown in Table 4.2, job enrichment is used widely and has gained in popularity since 1987. The broad acceptance of job enrichment probably results from the fact that this approach has been around for several decades and has been widely publicized (see, for example, Herzberg, 1966; Hackman and Oldham, 1980). However, job enrichment programs generally affect 20 percent or less of the employees in the organizations where they have been adopted. This situation may reflect the fact that the writings concerning them have been targeted at routine assembly and clerical jobs.

Self-managing work teams and minibusiness units are used much less frequently than job enrichment programs. Self-managing work teams are used in 68 percent of the corporations, but they have been applied to only a small percentage of the workforce. A comparison of the 1987 and 1990 data shows a significant increase from 28 percent to 47 percent in the use of self-managing work teams; a comparison between 1990 and 1993 shows a further significant increase from 47 percent to 68 percent. Even though most companies don't have a large number of employees in teams, these are impressive increases. Installing them involves much more than creating a temporary parallel structure. In many cases, equipment must be moved, employees trained, supervisors reassigned, and a host of other changes made. Despite these difficulties, significant change has occurred, leaving little question that real increases in power sharing are occurring in the Fortune 1000 companies and that teams are an increasingly popular approach to organizing and managing work.

Minibusiness units are used less frequently than any of the other power-sharing practices and, like the others, tend to affect a small percentage of the organization's employees. Nevertheless the results show a significant increase in the use of minibusiness units from 1990 to 1993. This finding is not unexpected given the increase in other power-sharing approaches, but it is a departure from the lack of change between 1987 and 1990. This approach involves more power sharing and change than do self-managing teams (Mills, 1991). The increased popularity of minibusiness units may mean that an increasing number of organizations are expanding their horizons with respect to restructuring and are going beyond self-managing teams to higher levels of involvement (Lawler, 1992). This interpretation is consistent with the finding that 65 percent of the companies have employee committees that focus on policy and strategy issues. Done effectively, this approach can give employees input in issues of organization-wide effectiveness.

Additional analysis of the data suggests that companies with job enrichment, self-managing work teams, and minibusiness units are more likely to have parallel structure activities such as quality circles. In other words, companies that engage in one of the more popular employee involvement activities are more likely to try the others. Table 4.3 shows, however, that use of multiple approaches on a large scale is not widespread. Only 37 percent of companies have tried two or more of these approaches with over 40 percent of their employees. Even though this represents a significant increase from 1990, it is still a low figure. Thus, although most companies are doing something to move power downward, very few companies are using an organization-wide approach or multiple approaches so that most employees will be affected by them.

Figure 4.1 shows that decision-making power increasingly has been moved to lower levels as a result of the involvement activities in these companies. This result fits with the popularity of the suggestion-oriented approaches and the increased popularity of job enrichment and work teams.

The data on activities designed to move power downward show that suggestion-type programs continue to be particularly widely

Table 4.3	Percentage of Companies Using Power-Sharing Approaches with More Than 40 Percent of Employees.		
NUMBER OF APPROACHES	1987 (N=323)	1990 (N=313)	1993 (N=279)
0	58	52	33
1	23	28	30
2	11	13	17
3	6	4	12
4	3	3	5
5 or more	0	1	3

Seven possible kinds: survey feedback, job enrichment, quality circles, employee participation groups, union-management QWL committees, minibusiness units, self-managing work teams.

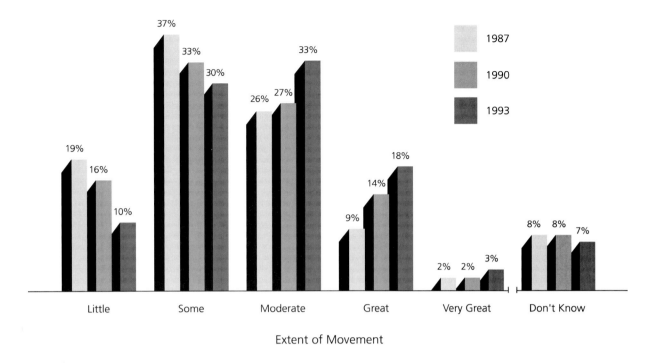

Legend:
- 1987
- 1990
- 1993

Little: 19%, 16%, 10%
Some: 37%, 33%, 30%
Moderate: 26%, 27%, 33%
Great: 9%, 14%, 18%
Very Great: 2%, 2%, 3%
Don't Know: 8%, 8%, 7%

Extent of Movement

Figure 4.1. Percentage Indicating Extent to Which Decision Making Moved to Lower Levels as a Result of Employee Involvement.

used. Most corporations have at least tried this approach somewhere. The reason is probably that these programs are the easiest to install and effect the least change in the power relationships in organizations. The growth of self-managing teams and minibusiness units is a very significant change and indicates that a number of companies are going beyond problem-solving approaches.

Finally, it is important to note that none of the power-sharing practices in Tables 4.1 and 4.2 are employed throughout most companies. Typically they cover fewer than 40 percent of the employees in the companies that utilize them. This finding strongly suggests that companies are piloting these practices or using them selectively rather than adopting them as organization-wide approaches to organizing and managing. In the case of some practices, this decision undoubtedly is appropriate since they are not universally applicable. Nevertheless it suggests that many companies are still not committed to creating high-involvement work organizations.

SECTION 5

Patterns of Information, Knowledge, Rewards, and Power

Scholars and managers alike recognize that employee behavior is determined by many forces in complex organizations. If managers want to develop a high level of employee involvement, it is simplistic to ask whether they should use power-sharing practices *or* reward practices *or* information sharing *or* training programs. All of these are needed. Interrelated patterns of mutually reinforcing practices are necessary to encourage and sustain employee behavior. The overall pattern of management practices is much more important than the use of any one practice.

In our 1990 study of Fortune 1000 firms (Lawler, Mohrman, and Ledford, 1992), we examined patterns of employee involvement (EI) practices that emerged from the data. Using a statistical technique called cluster analysis, we found that organizations using one practice tended to use all other practices to the same degree. Low users tended to be relatively low in their use of all practices, average users tended to be average in use of all practices, and high users tended to be high in the use of all practices. A fourth type, reward-oriented users, was different. These firms were high in use of rewards and quality practices but average in the use of other practices. This study takes a different approach. It examines the patterns of employee involvement practices used within firms by asking specifically about them. We studied three EI types (Lawler, 1988).

Suggestion involvement entails the power to make suggestions for change but not the power to make decisions. Suggestion involvement usually is provided by means of parallel structures, such as improvement teams or participation groups, that supplement rather than replace existing structures. The teams depend on the existing management structure for the implementation of changes they suggest. Although team members usually receive training, information, and recognition or rewards, such practices typically are not extended to employees in the unit who are not team members. As a result, this form of EI can be installed with relatively minor changes to the existing organization. In this sense, it is a limited type of involvement.

Job involvement is based on changes in work design, so that employees have more control over day-to-day decisions relevant to their jobs. These changes are accomplished through the enrichment of individual jobs or the creation of self-managing work teams for interdependent groups. One key organization design element—namely, work design—is automatically changed in this approach.

Information sharing, training, and rewards may also be changed to support the new work design.

Business involvement encompasses job involvement and suggestion involvement but goes further; it stresses the involvement of employees in managing the business. High-involvement organizations use a wide variety of mutually reinforcing design elements to support and facilitate employee involvement. Such organizations may use a wide variety of innovative power-sharing, information-sharing, skill-building, reward, and other human resource practices. The best-known examples are showcase manufacturing plants built by such companies as Procter & Gamble, General Mills, Anheuser-Busch, and many others. The term *high performance organization* is often applied to this type, but so far research evidence of a clear performance advantage for this type has been limited. It is also called a high-involvement design.

We investigated the use of these forms of employee involvement by asking respondents to the 1993 survey to answer the following question: "Approximately what percent of your corporation's employees are in units in which each of the following patterns of employee involvement practice is predominate?" Respondents were asked to allocate 100 percent of the workforce to one of five types, displayed in Table 5.1. The reader may note that we used the label "Improvement Teams" instead of "Suggestion Involvement" because past reactions of some managers suggested that the latter might elicit a negative reaction. We added another category, "Other Form of Involvement," to capture kinds of employee involvement and combinations of employee involvement practices that did not fit our classification system.

The average firm had no significant EI activities in units covering 37 percent of employees. Improvement teams were used in units covering 31 percent of employees, job involvement in units covering 12 percent of employees, and business involvement in units covering 10 percent of employees. Other forms of involvement covered 9 percent. This result is consistent with the view that there are no EI activities covering a significant portion of the U.S. workforce and that the most complex and intense forms (job involvement and business involvement) still cover only a relatively small part of the workforce. However, it does show that the average employee is likely to experience some form of involvement.

There was tremendous variation in the use of the involvement types from one firm to another. For this reason, we looked for a way to classify firms according to the pattern of involvement that

Table 5.1	Descriptions: Employee Involvement Types.
None	No significant employee involvement exists in these parts of the corporation.
Improvement Teams	Employee involvement focuses on special groups that are responsible for recommending improvements to management. These groups may be participation groups, quality circles, quality action teams, union-management QWL committees, etc. Members of the groups receive special training to enable them to work better as a team. They receive information relevant to the problems they are working on. There may be financial rewards or recognition for team suggestions.
Job Involvement	Employee involvement focuses on creating work designs that are highly motivating, such as self-managing teams. Training concentrates on job-specific skills and/or team functioning. Employees receive information relevant to their performance as individuals and/or teams. The reward system may reinforce the job design emphasis; practices might include team performance incentives or pay increases for mastering skills that are needed within a team.
Business Involvement	Employees are involved heavily in the management of the business. Improvement teams and job involvement approaches may be used as part of this strategy. Self-managing work teams and perhaps minibusiness units are used extensively, and management routinely seeks employee input on policies and practices of the organization. Reward innovations are used, perhaps including gainsharing or profit sharing in the unit. Employees receive extensive training in job skills, team skills, and business issues. Employees receive extensive business information, and they are expected to use it.
Other Form of Involvement	Employee involvement approaches not described above.

they emphasized. Inspection of the data suggested a relatively simple classification procedure that worked for all but twelve companies in our sample. This classification scheme is displayed in Table 5.2. We classified any company that did not cover at least half of the workforce in any form of EI as "Low Employee Involvement." A firm that covered at least a third of its employees in improvement teams was classified as emphasizing "Suggestion Involvement." A firm covering at least a third of its employees in job involvement, business involvement, or other involvement forms was classified as using that form.

Although the threshold of one-third of the workforce for classification in four of the types may seem low, the average firm in each category actually included a majority of its employees in that type. The average firm in the "Other" and "Business Involvement" types covered 53 percent of employees in units using those types of employee involvement. The average firm in the "Job Involvement"

Table 5.2	Classification of Firms by Employee Involvement Type.

EMPLOYEE INVOLVEMENT TYPE	Firm Classified as This Type if Percent of Employees Is Greater Than or Equal to:	Number of Companies	Percent of Sample
Low Employee Involvement	50% in no significant involvement effort	106	38%
Suggestion Involvement	33% in improvement teams	104	37%
Job Involvement	33% in job involvement	18	6%
Business Involvement	33% in business involvement	18	6%
Other Type of Involvement	33% in other type of involvement	21	8%
Not Classified	N/A	12	4%

type covered 58 percent with that form; the average firm in the "Suggestion Involvement" type covered 62 percent; the average firm in the "None" category covered 78 percent with the Low Involvement type.

Table 5.2 indicates that by far the two largest categories are Low Involvement and Suggestion Involvement, with 38 percent and 37 percent of firms respectively. This means that over a third of Fortune 1000 firms have made no major commitment to employee involvement, and a similar number emphasize the form of employee involvement that requires the least organizational change. Six percent of the firms in the sample fall into the Job Involvement and Business Involvement types, and 8 percent fall into the Other type. Again, this result is consistent with our experience and with data from prior studies indicating that the more complex, deeper forms of employee involvement are less common.

The remainder of this section examines the use of specific EI practices by companies representing each of the five types. Part of the data we report are indices, or summary scores, for information sharing, knowledge, reward, and power-sharing practices. The indices represent a composite measure of the degree to which companies are using various practices in each category. We also report scores for an index that is a combination of the other four indices. Resource C provides details on how these scores are calculated.

Information Sharing. Table 5.3 presents the results for information sharing. The Low Involvement firms share all kinds of information less than other types, and have the lowest index score. Business Involvement firms share the most information on corporate operating results, new technologies, business plans, and goals. The Business Involvement firms also receive the highest score on the index of information-sharing items. The Suggestion Involvement firms and Job Involvement firms share more information than the Low Involvement type overall. Job Involvement firms provide more information than other types concerning unit operating results. The Other Involvement firms are relatively high in information sharing, especially concerning corporate operating results.

Table 5.3	Mean Use of Information-Sharing Practices by Employee Involvement Type.

INFORMATION-SHARING PRACTICE	Low Involvement	Suggestion Involvement	Job Involvement	Business Involvement	Other Involvement
Corporate Operating Results	5.6	5.9	5.9	6.4	6.4
Unit Operating Results	4.5	5.2	6.1	5.8	5.1
New Technologies	3.6	3.8	4.2	4.6	4.4
Business Plans/Goals	4.3	4.8	5.4	5.6	4.8
Competitors' Performance	3.2	3.4	4.4	4.3	3.9
Information Index	**4.2**	**4.5**	**4.5**	**5.3**	**4.9**

Notes:
1. Numbers are mean responses to percent of employees covered by practice, using the following response scale:
   1 = None (0%),   2 = Almost none (1–20%),   3 = Some (21–40%),   4 = About half (41–60%),   5 = Most (61–80%),   6 = Almost all (81–99%),   7 = All (100%).

2. Analysis of variance test is significant for all practices except corporate operating results, indicating significant differences between one or more EI types and the grand mean.

Even the Low Involvement firms share a significant amount of information. The index score for this type corresponds to sharing information with about half of the workforce. However, the gap between the highest and lowest types on information sharing is substantial, representing a difference of about 20 percent of the workforce receiving information.

Knowledge. As shown in Table 5.4, the same general pattern that exists for information sharing also holds for training practices. Low Involvement firms cover the smallest percentage of employees with every type of training and have the lowest index score. The Business Involvement firms have the highest score for six of the seven types of training. Only for group decision-making

| Table 5.4 | Mean Use of Training by Employee Involvement Type. |

TRAINING PRACTICE	Low Involvement	Suggestion Involvement	Job Involvement	Business Involvement	Other Involvement
Group Decision-Making/ Problem-Solving Skills	2.6	3.6	3.8	3.7	3.2
Leadership Skills	2.6	3.2	3.3	3.8	3.0
Skills in Understanding the Business	2.3	2.6	3.2	3.3	2.4
Quality/Statistical Analysis Skills	2.6	3.9	3.8	4.1	3.3
Team-Building Skills	2.7	3.9	4.2	4.2	3.3
Job-Skills Training	4.0	4.5	4.8	4.9	4.1
Cross-Training	2.8	3.3	3.8	3.9	2.9
Training Index	**2.5**	**3.3**	**3.1**	**3.8**	**2.9**

Notes:
1. Numbers are mean responses to percent of employees covered by practice, using the following response scale:
   1 = None (0%), 2 = Almost none (1–20%), 3 = Some (21–40%), 4 = About half (41–60%), 5 = Most (61–80%), 6 = Almost all (81–99%), 7 = All (100%).

2. Analysis of variance test is significant for all practices, indicating significant differences between one or more EI types and the grand mean.

and problem-solving training is the mean higher for another type (Job Involvement), and that mean is only slightly higher. Suggestion Involvement, Job Involvement, and Other Involvement firms provide an intermediate level of training. Job Involvement firms tend to provide more job-skills training, cross-training, and even more group decision-making and problem-solving training than Suggestion Involvement firms. This finding is consistent with the skill needs of enriched job designs and self-managing work teams. Again the gap between the lowest and highest types is substantial. The difference between the Low Involvement and Business Involvement firms is over a point on the response scale, which corresponds to training for approximately 20 percent of the workforce.

Rewards. The pattern for reward practices shown in Table 5.5 is more complex than for information and training practices. Business Involvement firms provide more than any other EI type for nine of twelve reward practices. They make less use of work-group or team incentives than Job Involvement firms, are tied with Other Involvement firms in the use of all-salaried systems, and are lower than both Low Involvement and Other Involvement firms in the use of stock options.

Job Involvement firms tend to be relatively heavy users of all-salaried pay systems, skill-based pay systems, profit sharing, gainsharing, work-group or team incentives, open pay information, and employee stock options. All of these practices except stock options are consistent with prescriptions in the literature for reward systems that specifically support work teams. Suggestion Involvement firms are not heavy users of any type of reward practice, compared to other EI types. Other Involvement firms are heavy users of all-salaried systems, individual incentives, recognition rewards, and stock options. This result is consistent with a lack of emphasis on the use of monetary rewards by many advocates of quality circles, quality teams, and some other types of participation groups. Low Involvement firms make relatively heavy use only of stock options.

Our index for reward practices covers a subset of practices that the research literature indicates are especially relevant to employee involvement: knowledge- or skill-based pay, profit sharing, gainsharing, and employee stock ownership plans. The differences in the reward index scores are especially dramatic. The gap between the lowest type, Low Involvement, and the highest type, Business Involvement, is almost two full points, corresponding to coverage of about 40 percent more of the workforce in the Business Involvement firms.

Table 5.5

Mean Use of Reward Practices by Employee Involvement Type.

REWARD PRACTICE	Low Involvement	Suggestion Involvement	Job Involvement	Business Involvement	Other Involvement
All-Salaried Pay Systems	3.0	3.1	3.8	4.1	4.1
Knowledge/Skill-Based Pay	1.7	2.0	2.8	3.6	2.5
Profit Sharing	2.9	3.5	3.6	4.7	2.8
Gainsharing	1.4	1.9	2.8	2.9	2.0
Individual Incentives	2.7	2.9	3.0	3.5	3.3
Work-Group or Team Incentives	2.1	2.2	4.0	3.0	2.9
Nonmonetary Recognition Awards	3.6	4.6	4.9	5.3	4.9
Employee Stock Ownership Plan	3.6	4.3	4.4	5.3	3.9
Flexible, Cafeteria-Style Benefits	3.9	3.9	3.1	4.9	4.3
Employment Security	2.0	2.4	2.2	3.2	2.3
Open Pay Information	3.2	3.1	5.1	5.5	3.4
Stock Option Plan	2.7	2.5	2.8	2.6	2.8
Reward Index	**2.3**	**2.9**	**3.2**	**4.2**	**2.8**

Notes:
1. Numbers are mean responses to percent of employees covered by practice, using the following response scale:
   1 = None (0%), 2 = Almost none (1–20%), 3 = Some (21–40%), 4 = About half (41–60%), 5 = Most (61–80%), 6 = Almost all (81–99%), 7 = All (100%).

2. Analysis of variance test is significant for all practices except individual incentives, cafeteria benefits, and stock option plans, indicating significant differences between one or more EI types and the grand mean.

Power Sharing. Table 5.6 presents the results for power-sharing practices. Both the Low Involvement and Other Involvement types are relatively low in their use of power-sharing practices. The Low Involvement firms are lower in the use of every form of power sharing than any other type and have the lowest index score. The

POWER-SHARING PRACTICE	Low Involvement	Suggestion Involvement	Job Involvement	Business Involvement	Other Involvement
Suggestion System	3.1	3.8	3.9	4.8	3.6
Survey Feedback	3.3	4.5	4.8	5.4	4.8
Job Enrichment or Redesign	2.0	2.7	4.1	3.9	2.7
Quality Circles	1.8	2.9	2.7	2.2	2.1
Employee Participation Groups Other Than Quality Circles	2.4	4.0	3.6	4.2	2.8
Union-Management QWL Committees	1.3	1.9	2.3	2.0	1.4
Minibusiness Units	1.5	1.8	2.5	3.2	2.2
Self-Managing Work Teams	1.6	2.1	2.6	2.2	2.0
Employee Committees Concerned with Policy and/or Strategy	1.6	2.1	2.1	2.9	1.9
Power-Sharing Index	**2.0**	**2.8**	**2.9**	**3.2**	**2.5**

Notes:
1. Numbers are mean responses to percent of employees covered by practice, using the following response scale:
   1 = None (0%), 2 = Almost none (1–20%), 3 = Some (21–40%), 4 = About half (41–60%), 5 = Most (61–80%), 6 = Almost all (81–99%), 7 = All (100%).

2. Analysis of variance test is highly significant for all practices, indicating significant differences between one or more EI types and the grand mean.

Other Involvement firms make relatively heavy use of survey feedback but otherwise are moderate in their use of power-sharing practices (as they should be if our classification is accurate). The Suggestion Involvement, Job Involvement, and Business Involvement firms are high in practices that are most relevant to their types. The Suggestion Involvement firms are relatively heavy users of quality circles, employee participation groups, and union-management QWL committees. The Job Involvement firms are the highest in the use of job enrichment and self-managing work teams. Surprisingly, they are highest in the use of union-management QWL committees, and they make relatively heavy use of quality circles. The Business Involvement firms have the highest index score and also the highest scores for use of employee committees concerned with policy and strategy, minibusiness units, survey feedback, and suggestion systems. These firms also are the highest in the use of participation groups and are relatively heavy users of union-management QWL committees and self-managing teams.

The Job Involvement and Business Involvement organizations make use of practices associated with Suggestion Involvement as well as others that may require greater organizational change. This result is consistent with the observation that firms often evolve from suggestion involvement to job or business involvement, while maintaining older forms of involvement in the process. It is also possible that these firms emphasize suggestion involvement in some parts of the company and job or business involvement in other parts.

The gap between the high and low types is significant. For some specific practices such as survey feedback, job enrichment, and participation groups, the differences between the Low Involvement type and the highest score types is about two points on our response scale. This corresponds to a difference of about 40 percent of the workforce being covered by power-sharing practices.

Overall Use of EI Practices. We can summarize differences in the overall use of EI practices among the five types by considering their scores on the overall index of EI practices. The EI index score for Business Involvement firms is the highest, at 4.1. This score means that the average Business Involvement firm covers 41 to 60 percent of the workforce with the typical EI practice. The EI index scores for the Other Involvement (3.3), Suggestion Involvement (3.2), and Job Involvement (3.1) firms are similar. These represent coverage of 21 to 40 percent of employees in these firms with the typical EI practice. Finally, the EI index score for Low Involvement firms is 2.6, representing a coverage of between 1 and 20 percent of the workforce with the typical EI practice.

Several different approaches to employee involvement emerge from our analysis. The Low Involvement firms consistently make relatively low use of information, training, reward, and power-sharing practices. This does not mean that firms in this category use no employee involvement practices. They tend to employ all of them to some degree but make significantly less use of them than other types. The Suggestion Involvement, Job Involvement, and Business Involvement firms are consistent with our expectations about the practices they use. It is interesting that the Job Involvement and Business Involvement types seem to make relatively heavy use of the practices that are associated with Suggestion Involvement. No clear picture of the Other Involvement type emerges from our analysis. Further inspection of specific cases indicates that firms in this type use a variety of idiosyncratic patterns rather than one homogenous pattern.

PART TWO

Adoption of Total Quality Management

Adopting Total Quality Programs and Practices

Total quality management (TQM) is a set of organizational strategies, practices, and tools for organizational performance improvement. The theoretical relationship between employee involvement and TQM is readily apparent. EI describes organizational design features that characterize highly participative organizations. TQM describes a philosophy of organizational improvement and approaches that its advocates argue cannot be successful without employee involvement (Deming, 1986). This section describes current patterns of adoption of TQM practices; the next section will explore the relationship between EI and TQM.

A variety of practices are included under the general rubric of TQM. At the operational level, it includes application of systematic approaches to the measurement and improvement of work processes to ensure that they are adding value and meeting the needs of the customer. Work simplification is often part and parcel of TQM, as organizations focus on eliminating steps that do not add value and on combining tasks to reduce the number of interfaces.

Many companies are collaborating with their suppliers in the efforts to improve quality. They recognize that quality problems often result from the delivery of supplies and raw material that do not meet process specifications, and that the supplier interfaces often entail non-value-added steps. Although the focus is primarily on *quality*, defined as meeting the needs of the customer, TQM also has cost, service, and schedule implications. The practice of monitoring the cost of quality links the quality and customer-focused aspects of TQM to the financial-cost aspects of the organization. In order to create customer focus, TQM often includes systematic customer satisfaction monitoring and direct exposure of employees to customers to ensure an understanding of their needs and to reinforce the customer focus.

TQM was first applied in manufacturing settings, where it typically includes training front-line employees to use statistical process control methods to monitor and improve work processes and to inspect their own work. It also often includes just-in-time deliveries from suppliers to reduce inventory costs. Some organizations have redesigned the workplace into work cells, which apply TQM techniques and in many cases have the characteristics of self-managing teams. These approaches are also applied in some of the more production-oriented parts of the administrative and service areas of organizations.

TQM also includes strategic elements—for example, involving management in quality councils that link TQM activities to the key strategic focuses of the organization, and using cross-functional planning that explicitly acknowledges and plans for interdependencies between functions in improving the processes of an organization. A recent change program that is related to TQM is reengineering (for example, Hammer and Champy, 1993; Davenport, 1993). Faithfully executed, this is an approach that takes a fundamental look at the mission of the organization vis-à-vis its customers and the way it organizes to conduct that mission. It may result in the introduction of substantially different work processes. Rather than take the process-improvement approach that is common in TQM, reengineering focuses on reconceptualizing the work that is done and how it is done, often by incorporating the capabilities of information technology. In practice, reengineering often equates to process simplification and lateral integration with a primary focus on downsizing.

Since the early 1980s, the use of TQM approaches has been on an upward trajectory in U.S. companies. In our 1993 survey, 76 percent of companies reported having a TQM program (see Table 6.1). This compares with 73 percent in our 1990 survey and with 74 percent reported in a 1993 survey of human resource and quality respondents (Moran, Hogeveen, Latham, and Ross-Eft, 1994). A study of the Business Roundtable corporate quality officers conducted by Delta Consulting (1993) found that 14 percent had no company wide quality effort and another 17 percent were at the initial stages.

Table 6.1	Total Quality Management Coverage.		
		1990	1993
Percent of Companies with a TQM Program		73%	76%
Average Percent of Employees Covered		41%	50%
Percent of Companies with 100% of Employees Covered		18%	25%

Table 6.2 shows that 81 percent of the TQM programs reported in our study began after 1985. The fact that 24 percent of the programs began after 1991 but that the overall percentage of companies using TQM rose only 3 percent during the period between 1990 and 1993 (well within the error margin for our study) means that some of the Fortune 1000 have dropped their TQM programs as well. Nevertheless usage continues in approximately three-quarters of the largest U.S. companies.

The breadth of use of TQM practices may also be increasing in Fortune 1000 companies. In our 1993 survey, TQM programs on average covered 50 percent of employees, compared with 41 percent in our 1990 survey. One-quarter of companies (compared to 18 percent in 1990) report that all employees are covered by TQM programs. Furthermore, 83 percent of the companies report increased or greatly increased use of TQM over the past three years (Table 6.3). This result may reflect the migration of TQM from the factory floor, where it originated, to other parts of the organization.

Attention has been focused on TQM in part by the giving of prestigious awards to companies with exemplary quality programs. In the United States, the most visible is the Malcolm Baldrige National Quality Award. Eighteen percent of our respondents report having competed for this award. Of those, 76 percent report that the competition was a positive or very positive experience. Although the prestige of winning is no doubt one motivation for competing, many companies also take part because they find the TQM model embedded in the Baldrige criteria to be a useful road map. As a result, they welcome the discipline of systematically evaluating themselves according to those criteria. A number of U.S. companies have also competed for and several have won the prestigious Deming Award, which is given in Japan. In addition,

Table 6.2	Year That Total Quality Programs Began.
Prior to 1986	19%
1986 – 1988	25%
1989 – 1990	32%
1991 – 1993	24%

Table 6.3	Change in Use of TQM Over the Past Three Years.
Greatly Decreased	3.3%
Decreased	2.8%
Stayed the Same	10.8%
Increased	63.7%
Greatly Increased	19.3%

a number of similar state-based awards have sprung up, and many companies are employing a similar evaluation and award system internally among their various operating units.

The proliferation of TQM-oriented consulting resources has also been a factor supporting its rapid growth. Although many companies build and develop internal consulting capabilities in the arena of TQM, 61 percent of our 1993 respondents report having used external consultants. External consultants frequently help a company develop the internal capabilities to sustain TQM practices and philosophy. Of those, 73 percent report having had a positive or very positive experience with these consultants.

Table 6.4 presents usage patterns for a number of common TQM practices. This table includes data from companies indicating that they have TQM programs; when available, 1990 data is presented to show changes in usage patterns. These practices are presented in three groupings that are the results of a statistical analysis to determine common usage patterns. The first seven practices are the core practices that tend to be adopted by most companies as they become increasingly involved in TQM. The four production-oriented practices are so labeled because they constitute a related set of efforts that are adopted primarily in production settings. These practices tend to be used where the work is routine and measurable, most frequently in manufacturing settings, but also in white-collar throughput-oriented environments. The patterns of adoption for each of the last two practices do not relate to each other or to the preceding two clusters of practices. They are treated as individual practices in all analyses.

Table 6.4

Percentage of Employees Covered by Total Quality Practices.

TQM PRACTICES	Mean	None (0%)	Almost None (1–20%)	Some (21–40%)	About Half (41–60%)	Most (61–80%)	Almost All (81–99%)	All (100%)
Core Practices								
Quality Improvement Teams	3.88	3	21	20	22	14	15	5
Quality Councils	2.95	20	35	14	12	5	8	5
Cross-Functional Planning	2.82	13	38	26	8	10	4	2
Process Reengineering	3.04	8	35	30	11	8	4	4
Work Simplification	3.23 (3.02)	8 (13)	28 (26)	28 (33)	17 (12)	8 (7)	6 (7)	4 (0)
Customer Satisfaction Monitoring	4.23	1	15	25	18	13	18	10
Direct Employee Exposure to Customers	3.29 (3.11)	2 (4)	31 (32)	33 (31)	16 (16)	11 (4)	6 (4)	2 (0)
Production-Oriented Practices								
Self-Inspection	3.38 (3.19)	7 (10)	27 (25)	27 (31)	14 (14)	15 (7)	8 (7)	3 (0)
Statistical Control Method Used by Front-Line Employees	2.82	12	38	27	11	7	5	1
Just-in-Time Deliveries	2.88 (2.63)	17 (24)	29 (31)	26 (22)	13 (11)	8 (4)	6 (4)	1 (2)
Work Cells or Manufacturing Cells	2.23 (2.14)	35 (41)	33 (27)	14 (19)	14 (9)	3 (2)	2 (2)	0 (0)
Other Practices								
Cost-of-Quality Monitoring	2.78 (2.73)	17 (18)	37 (35)	20 (24)	13 (11)	6 (4)	5 (4)	2 (3)
Collaboration with Suppliers in Quality Efforts	3.39 (2.80)	5 (13)	28 (37)	27 (27)	16 (11)	13 (3)	8 (3)	3 (2)

(1990 percentages in parentheses if available; N = 206)

The use of work simplification and direct exposure to customers was measured in 1990 and 1993; a comparison shows that both have increased. Two-thirds of the companies with TQM programs use these practices in areas with more than 20 percent of the workforce. The two most heavily used core practices are quality improvement teams and customer satisfaction monitoring. Four-fifths of companies use customer satisfaction monitoring in areas covering more than 20 percent of the workforce, and 18 percent cover all employees with this practice. Three-quarters use quality improvement teams with more than 20 percent of the workforce, and 15 percent cover all employees.

The less frequently used practices include quality councils, cross-functional planning, and process reengineering. Fewer than 60 percent of companies use them in areas that cover more than 20 percent of the workforce. It is significant that these less frequently employed practices are those that are more strategic in nature and involve higher-level direction and involvement.

The three production-oriented practices that were measured at two points in time all experienced small increases. The most frequently used is self-inspection, a practice used by two-thirds of companies with more than 20 percent of employees. Statistical process control by front-line employees and just-in-time deliveries are used by about half of the companies in areas covering more than 20 percent of the employees. The least frequently employed practice is work cells; these are not used at all by 35 percent of companies and are employed by only one-third of companies with more than 20 percent of employees.

The relatively low usage pattern of the production-oriented practices no doubt reflects the fact that they are not applicable in the parts of a company that do not perform production-oriented work. Use of these practices may in fact cover a large percentage of the applicable employees, given that fewer than 35 percent of employees in these companies are involved in manufacturing operations.

The use of cost-of-quality monitoring increased negligibly. Fewer than half the companies use it with more than 20 percent of their employees. By contrast, collaboration with suppliers in quality efforts experienced the largest and most significant overall gain of any practice. Two-thirds of companies used this with more than 20 percent of their employees, up from one-half of the companies in the 1990 survey. The increased implementation of this practice is particularly interesting because it includes two or more organizations.

The 1993 survey results show that three-quarters of companies have TQM programs, and a majority report an increase in TQM activity. The findings suggest a small increase in TQM activities from 1990 to 1993. The number of companies with programs did not significantly increase, but the amount of activity in companies with programs *did*. Usage patterns for particular practices vary considerably, with only a few companies employing any of the practices with all employees. On average, about half of employees are covered by some TQM practices. Quality improvement teams and customer satisfaction monitoring are the most extensively employed. Collaboration with suppliers is increasing the most rapidly. In general, the operational aspects of TQM are used most broadly. The strategic approaches that involve top-management involvement, such as the creation of quality councils and cross-functioning planning, are used less.

SECTION 7

Relationships Between Employee Involvement and Total Quality Programs

The similarities and differences between employee involvement and TQM are highlighted in Table 7.1 (see also Lawler, 1994). The employee involvement and TQM literatures share an emphasis on the use of participation groups that utilize problem-solving and decision-making tools. They both emphasize performance feedback and information sharing, although TQM tends to focus primarily on *process* feedback and customer information, whereas the employee involvement literature also focuses on *business* results and information. TQM provides management tools that emphasize the control and improvement of work processes and gears all activities to customer requirements. Employee involvement emphasizes the

Table 7.1	Comparison of EI and TQM.	
TQM EMPHASIS	**Shared Emphasis**	**EI Emphasis**
Process Management	Participation Groups	Aligning Motivational Systems:
Customer Orientation	Problem-Solving and Decision-Making Tools and Training	Job design Goal setting Appraisal Rewards
	Feedback	Work Unit Design
	Information Sharing	Business Involvement

motivational system in the organization, including the design of motivating jobs and ways of setting goals and reviewing and rewarding performance. It also focuses on the design of work units and business units to enable employee involvement in business success.

TQM and employee involvement can complement one another. TQM requires that the organization be designed and managed for involvement so that people can improve its performance. TQM provides tools and approaches to facilitate successful performance improvement and employee involvement. This section investigates the actual empirical relationship between the two approaches.

Figure 7.1 shows the relationship between TQM and EI programs. In 1993, 41 percent of companies said that their quality programs started first, whereas 37 percent said EI started first. The pattern was reversed in 1990, when EI programs were more likely to have started first. This somewhat puzzling result may reflect the fact that recently most organizational change efforts have started with a TQM emphasis.

Fifty-four percent of companies manage them as two integrated programs, and 25 percent coordinate them. The change in the percentage of companies managing them as an integrated program is particularly striking—up from 36 percent in 1990. Only 21 percent still manage them as two separate programs. Apparently companies are increasingly seeing the complementary and related nature of these two programs.

TQM is the primary focus. Eighty percent of companies see employee involvement as part of TQM, and only 20 percent see TQM as part of their EI initiatives. This finding provides evidence that many companies are adopting EI design elements to assist TQM activities rather than adopting TQM as a set of practices to channel and strengthen employee involvement.

There is a strong correlation between the adoption of employee involvement approaches and the use of TQM practices (see Table 7.2). The extent to which companies employ the core TQM practices, the production-oriented practices, collaboration with customers, and cost-of-quality monitoring all have a highly significant relationship to the overall employee involvement index. The relationship to the development of knowledge and skill is particularly strong, demonstrating the strong emphasis in TQM programs on the development of skills. TQM's relationship to power sharing is also very strong, reflecting the focus on problem-solving and decision-making groups in TQM in general and on work cells and teams.

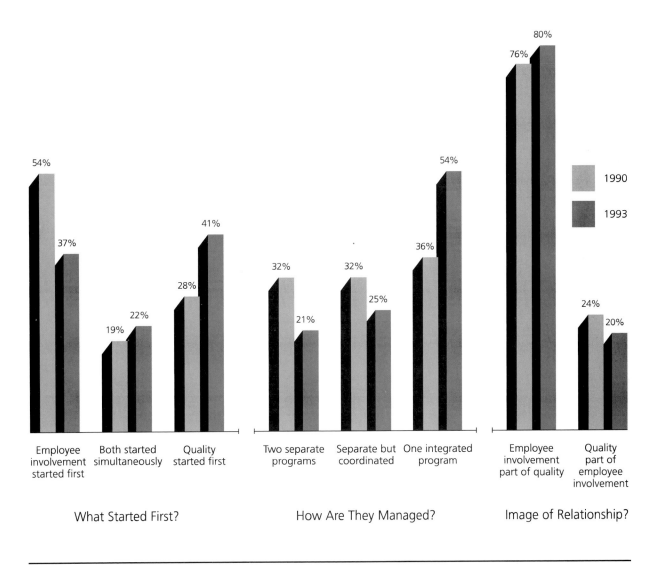

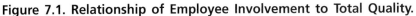

Figure 7.1. Relationship of Employee Involvement to Total Quality.

The relationship between TQM and information sharing is substantially weaker than the one for knowledge. Apparently many TQM programs are stressing training in the use of improvement tools and power sharing at the work-flow level but are not going beyond that to share important business information with employees. Most companies are staying at the level of suggestion and job involvement.

There is no significant relationship between the use of the core or production-oriented TQM practices and the sharing of performance-oriented rewards. The lack of a relationship to rewards suggests

Table 7.2

Relationship Between EI Indices and TQM.[1] (Correlation Coefficients)

TQM	EI Overall	Information Sharing	Knowledge and Skills Development	Power Sharing	Rewards
Core Practices Overall	**.41****	**.29****	**.50****	**.48****	**.13**
Quality Improvement Teams	.24**	.08	.32**	.32**	.11
Quality Councils	.20*	.12	.30**	.27**	.06
Cross-Functional Planning	.38**	.24**	.47**	.47**	.13
Process Reengineering	.29**	.22*	.34**	.34**	.04
Work Simplification	.38**	.23**	.44**	.38**	.18
Customer Satisfaction Monitoring	.35**	.32**	.38**	.41**	.06
Direct Employee Exposure to Customers	.30**	.31**	.36**	.34**	.08
Production-Oriented Practices Overall	**.39****	**.22****	**.51****	**.40****	**.16**
Self-Inspection	.36**	.21*	.42**	.34**	.20*
Statistical Control Method Used by Front-Line Employees	.36**	.16	.47**	.36**	.11
Just-in-Time Deliveries	.25*	.19*	.38**	.23*	.13
Work Cells or Manufacturing Cells	.28**	.13	.37**	.34**	.08
Other Practices					
Cost-of-Quality Monitoring	.34*	.22*	.36**	.32**	.17
Collaboration with Suppliers in Quality Efforts	.39**	.26**	.47**	.41**	.11
Percent of Employees Involved	**.28****	**.12**	**.35****	**.35****	**.05**

1. See Resource C for explanation of indices.

Key: * = moderate relationship (p≤ .01)
       ** = strong relationship (p≤.001)

that companies that employ TQM are not making employees stakeholders in business performance. As can be seen in Table 7.2, the percentage of employees covered by TQM is related to the overall amount of employee involvement but not to the use of rewards or to information sharing. TQM for most employees does not appear to mean a business partnership.

Only one of the individual TQM practices, self-inspection, is significantly related to the reward index. Companies that are eliminating multiple inspections and promoting self-inspection seem to be more likely to link rewards to performance. Another interesting finding is that work simplification is positively related to power sharing and to knowledge and skills development. It would appear that simplification is not leading inexorably to simple, unenriched jobs; quite the opposite appears to be true. Self-inspection, often a part of work simplification, is also accompanied by knowledge and skill development and power sharing.

Another interesting finding is the strong relationship of cross-functional planning to the EI indices. The creation of planning processes that extend across the organization appears to result in more opportunities for people to be informed about their company, develop knowledge and skills to make a difference, and participate in empowered decision-making forums.

Table 7.3 shows the patterns of adoption of TQM practices by companies with the different employee involvement types discussed

Table 7.3 — **Use of Quality Practices by Different Employee Involvement (EI) Types.[1]**

		EMPLOYEE INVOLVEMENT TYPE			
TQM	None	Suggestion Involvement	Job Involvement	Business Involvement	Other (unspecified)
Core Practices Overall	**2.7**	**3.6**	**3.9**	**4.5**	**3.1**
Quality Improvement Teams	2.8	4.5	3.9	4.7	3.8
Quality Councils	2.3	3.4	2.8	4.4	2.0
Cross-Functional Planning	2.1	3.0	3.5	4.1	2.8
Process Reengineering	2.5	3.2	4.2	4.1	3.1
Work Simplification	2.5	3.4	4.6	4.7	3.2
Customer Satisfaction Monitoring	3.7	4.5	4.7	5.5	4.1
Direct Employee Exposure to Customers	3.1	3.3	3.4	4.5	3.1
Production-Oriented Practices Overall	**2.3**	**3.0**	**3.3**	**3.5**	**2.6**
Self-Inspection	2.6	3.7	4.2	4.6	3.4
Statistical Control Method Used by Front-Line Employees	2.3	3.2	2.9	3.1	2.6
Just-In-Time Deliveries	2.6	3.1	3.0	3.9	2.5
Work Cells or Manufacturing Cells	1.8	2.3	3.0	2.5	1.9
Other Practices					
Cost-of-Quality Monitoring	2.2	3.0	3.9	3.5	2.4
Collaboration with Suppliers in Quality Efforts	2.7	3.8	3.7	4.2	3.1

[1]Mean score on a scale from 1 – 7.

in Section 5. Companies with the more complex and complete form of employee involvement—business involvement—are also highest in the use of the core and production-oriented approaches to TQM. They are also higher in all but one of the core practices, as well as in the use of self-inspection, just-in-time deliveries, and collaboration with suppliers in total quality efforts. Business involvement entails employee participation that focuses on both the internal and the external aspects of the organization. This emphasis is mirrored in the kinds of TQM approaches utilized.

Companies that stress job involvement in their EI initiatives are highest on the related areas of work simplification, process reengineering, and work cells, all of which have job design ramifications. About 60 percent of these companies are primarily in manufacturing businesses. This result relates to the previously discussed pattern in Table 7.2, which suggests that simplification is not being used to de-skill jobs in many companies. Ideally the process reengineering and work cell approach will lead to work designs that give individuals and/or teams more responsibility and control over the work flow.

Companies with job involvement approaches to employee participation also are high on two measurement areas: customer satisfaction monitoring and cost-of-quality monitoring. One explanation for this finding is that good measurement systems enable the transfer of responsibility and authority and provide a foundation for management to use results to direct their companies instead of running day-to-day activities.

The most common type of employee participation is suggestion involvement. Companies that use suggestion involvement are also especially high in the use of quality improvement teams (although companies with a business involvement strategy use these teams more often than any others). Suggestion involvement relies primarily on these teams as a way of getting employees to participate, with less of a commitment to many of the other aspects of TQM. It does not constitute a complete organizational management and improvement strategy or employee involvement approach.

Companies that report having no employee involvement initiative covering the majority of their employees are those that also report the least TQM activity. Companies in the "other" category seem to employ quality improvement teams at a relatively high level. In most other categories, they are between companies with no employee involvement and those with a suggestion involvement approach. In many areas, they are significantly lower than job and particularly business involvement companies.

Although companies with no employee involvement are low in the application of TQM approaches, they employ them to some extent. They cover an average of about one-third of their employees with direct exposure to customers, which may be a natural part of providing service. More than half of their employees are in units where customer satisfaction is monitored. Of course, this may be an ongoing performance measure rather than an attempt to involve employees in performance improvement. Employee involvement may not be the intention, and it may not automatically result if employees do not systematically take part in addressing the measures and improving customer service. Furthermore, the use of these practices does not necessarily imply a formal TQM program.

Companies without employee involvement are using some of the other practices with more than 20 percent of their population. In these companies, it is likely that approaches like quality improvement teams may be the only or the primary way employees are able to participate in improvement activities and also that the organization does not encourage such participation.

Table 7.4 shows that companies not reporting any TQM activities do indicate some employee involvement activities. In some cases,

| Table 7.4 | EI Practices in Companies with and Without a TQM Program. |

EI MEASURES*	No TQM Program	TQM Program
EI Overall	11.98	13.08
Information-Sharing Index	4.37	4.61
Knowledge and Skills Development Index	2.67	3.13
Power-Sharing Index	2.21	2.63
Rewards Index	2.72	2.76
Quality Circles	1.70	2.48
Other Participation Groups	2.55	3.50

* Means are on a 1 (low) – 7 (high) scale with the exception of EI Overall, where they are on a 1–28 scale.

their level of EI is close to that of other companies. In particular, they share information with employees almost as much as companies with TQM. They employ performance-oriented rewards to the same extent as companies that have TQM. However, they develop knowledge and skills and share power significantly less than the entire sample. In addition, they employ both quality circles and other participation groups significantly less broadly than the typical company.

In sum, most companies have both employee involvement and TQM initiatives. They are most frequently coordinated or managed as one integrated program. Companies that have no EI applied to large parts of their population nevertheless have some TQM practices and vice versa. Suggestion involvement is widely used without the broad use of the other forms of involvement that would result in a more complete performance improvement-oriented organization. Companies with business involvement have the broadest application of almost all performance improvement approaches.

PART THREE

Results of Employee Involvement and TQM

Reward System Results

The reward-system practices most commonly associated with employee involvement were rated on their success in enhancing organizational performance. Table 8.1 presents the results concerning performance-based reward practices for 1990 and 1993 (these questions were not asked in the 1987 survey). Overall the ratings for 1993 are extremely positive and are very similar to those reported in 1990. All the pay-for-performance systems are rated as quite successful. No system was rated as unsuccessful by more than 7 percent of the companies, an impressively low rate of failure.

As was true in 1990, the highest success ratings for 1993 go to profit-sharing and employee stock ownership plans. These also are the plans that have been adopted for the longest period of time—an average of twelve years in the case of profit sharing and nine years in the case of employee stock ownership. Stock option plans are also rated as quite successful and have been around for an average of fourteen years. Apparently these plans are well established in the Fortune 1000 companies and clearly are rated very favorably. However, given their nature and when they were put in place, it is doubtful that they are an important part of companies' employee involvement and TQM programs.

Gainsharing is a much newer practice; the average company has used it for 3.2 years. Thus it is not surprising to find that more respondents are undecided with respect to its success. Nevertheless, 65 percent rated it as either successful or very successful, an increase from 54 percent in 1990. Only 7 percent rated it unsuccessful or very unsuccessful. This finding is generally in line with the results of other studies that have measured the quantitative success of gainsharing (see, for example, O'Dell, 1987; U.S. General Accounting Office, 1981). These studies tend to find success rates of 60 to 70 percent.

Work-group or team incentives are also rated as quite successful. Again there is a relatively large percentage of ratings in the undecided category, but few report failure. These programs have been around an average of five years. Given the increased use of teams during this time it is likely that some of these plans were created to support EI efforts.

The results for nonmonetary recognition rewards are also quite favorable. Seventy-five percent rate them as successful or very successful. These programs average thirteen years in use. Apparently most of them have not been introduced as part of a recent movement to employee involvement. Instead they represent well-established efforts to recognize outstanding employee performance in a wide range of areas. In some cases, of course, they may have been adapted and developed to help support an employee involvement or total quality effort.

Table 8.1 **Percentage Indicating Success of Performance-Based Reward Practices.**

		Very Unsuccessful	Unsuccessful	Undecided	Successful	Very Successful
Individual Incentives	1990	2	5	19	62	12
	1993	2	4	17	63	14
Work-Group or Team Incentives	1990	0	5	34	51	10
	1993	0	2	37	48	13
Profit Sharing	1990	0	4	25	45	26
	1993	1	3	21	44	30
Gainsharing	1990	1	3	43	42	12
	1993	2	5	30	47	17
Employee Stock Ownership Plan	1990	1	4	23	49	23
	1993	2	7	24	47	21
Stock Option Plan	1990			— — not asked — —		
	1993	2	4	18	57	19
Nonmonetary Recognition Awards for Performance	1990	0	2	18	63	17
	1993	1	1	22	59	17

Table 8.2 presents the results for EI-supportive reward-system practices. Companies reporting on all-salaried pay systems indicate a high level of success (76 percent). This result is similar to that in 1990. These are relatively well-established programs that have been in place an average of thirteen years.

Most knowledge- or skill-based pay programs are relatively new (an average of four years old), but nevertheless they seem to be working. Fifty-three percent of the companies report that their programs are a success. As was true in 1990, a relatively large number of respondents are undecided about the success of this practice. There is clear evidence that most of them were created to support EI efforts. They tend to be adopted by organizations that have recently installed self-managing teams.

The typical company has had a flexible benefit program a little less than five years. The reported success rate is very high, topping

Table 8.2		Percentage Indicating Success of EI-Supportive Reward Practices.				
		Very Unsuccessful	Unsuccessful	Undecided	Successful	Very Successful
All-Salaried Pay Systems	1990	0	2	23	59	17
	1993	2	6	16	63	13
Knowledge/Skill-Based Pay	1990	3	3	35	54	6
	1993	1	3	44	46	6
Flexible, Cafeteria-Style Benefits	1990	2	2	31	42	24
	1993	1	1	16	54	28
Employment Security	1990			— — not asked — —		
	1993	3	8	26	48	15
Open Pay Information	1990			— — not asked — —		
	1993	2	4	41	47	7

82 percent—a significant increase from 1990. This reward-system practice is obviously proving to be increasingly effective. One possible explanation for the high success rate is that even though most plans have been recently adopted (five years in use), considerable effort has been put into developing the technology of flexible benefits. A number of consulting firms have developed good plans, and as a result companies can move ahead with these programs without having to do a great deal of their own development work. Companies therefore can have a high probability of success when they adopt flexible benefit programs, even though they may be doing something that is new and different for them.

Employment security, which has been under attack in many companies, is rated as successful even so. The average age of these plans is eight years; not surprisingly, few have been started recently. It remains an open question whether some form of employment stability is necessary for a successful employee involvement or TQM program. A number of theorists have argued that it is important to it have it, but there is little or no evidence to support this assertion.

Finally, the ratings on open pay information are generally favorable. Like knowledge-based pay, there is a high percentage of undecided respondents, but only 6 percent describe it as being unsuccessful.

The overall results reported in Tables 8.1 and 8.2 are quite impressive. The respondents' clear feeling is that these reward-system practices are important contributors to organizational performance.

SECTION 9

Power-Sharing Results

Users of the power-sharing practices discussed in Section 4 were asked to evaluate their success in helping improve organizational performance. The results for those involving suggestion and problem-solving activities are summarized in Table 9.1. The pattern of responses for 1993 is very similar to the results obtained in our 1987 and 1990 studies. All of the programs are rated as successful or very successful by a majority of the respondents. No approach is rated unsuccessful by more than 14 percent of respondents, although a number of respondents indicated that they are undecided about the programs.

The most favorable ratings went to survey feedback and employee participation groups. As noted earlier, both of these approaches are parallel participation vehicles that take people out of their traditional work roles for discussions of how the workplace can

Table 9.1

Percentage Indicating Success of Suggestion Involvement Practices.

		Very Unsuccessful	Unsuccessful	Undecided	Successful	Very Successful
Quality Circles	1987	0	5	26	55	14
	1990	1	11	36	49	4
	1993	2	11	32	48	7
Employee Participation Groups Other Than QCs	1987	0	3	25	57	16
	1990	1	0	26	62	11
	1993	1	1	21	66	12
Union-Management QWL Committees	1987	0	8	42	44	6
	1990	0	2	48	46	4
	1993	2	5	39	49	6
Survey Feedback	1987	1	3	27	56	14
	1990	0	5	25	60	9
	1993	1	5	35	47	13
Suggestion Systems	1987			— — not asked — —		
	1990			— — not asked — —		
	1993	3	17	34	40	7

be improved. These programs require no fundamental change in the management style of the organization. They are relatively easy to implement in all kinds of organizations and, as research has shown, can produce positive results in most situations (Lawler, 1986). Thus their popularity and success are easy to understand.

Quality circles are seen as less successful than survey feedback and participation groups. This finding represents a significant change from 1987, when they were rated as comparable; however, it repeats the finding from 1990, which found them to be less successful. What explains the less-favorable ratings for quality circles? A number of articles and books have pointed out the transitory nature of their success and have warned that they may not be a good long-term approach to employee involvement (Lawler and Mohrman, 1985; Lawler, 1992). It seems that a number of companies are finding that this is true. In addition, during the middle 1980s, quality circles became a fad, and it is possible that some of the drop in their success rating is due to overuse and misuse.

Union-management quality of work life (QWL) committees also get relatively low success ratings. It should be noted that this lower rating is only relative; 55 percent of union-management QWL efforts were rated successful or very successful, and only 7 percent were rated unsuccessful. Typically they are the most complicated parallel structures to design, implement, and manage because they must be jointly run by unions and managements that previously have dealt with each other in a primarily adversarial mode (Herrick, 1990; Cohen-Rosenthal, 1995). Furthermore, many of these structures are being established in old-line unionized industries during very difficult economic times that involve downsizing, layoffs, and plant shutdowns and consolidations. Finally, dealing in a cooperative problem-solving way constitutes breaking important new ground and involves using and developing new skills. Success is by no means assured and may be difficult to obtain under these conditions.

Table 9.2 reports the results for work-restructuring practices. Job enrichment, work teams, minibusiness units, and policy and strategy committees often require major structural changes in other design elements of the organization (Wellins, Byham, and Wilson, 1991; Lawler, 1992). They therefore may be more difficult to implement and operate successfully than suggestion practices.

The companies that report having work-restructuring programs generally say that they are successful. Particularly impressive are the success rates reported for self-managing teams and minibusiness units. Both of these approaches are relatively new in most companies (four and three years old). The 1993 data show an increase in the degree to which minibusiness units are rated as successful, and they have the highest percentage of very successful ratings of any power-sharing practice. Apparently most of the companies that have adopted them have found them to be very good

Table 9.2 **Percentage Indicating Success of Work-Redesign Involvement Practices.**

		Very Unsuccessful	Unsuccessful	Undecided	Successful	Very Successful
Job Enrichment or Redesign	1987	0	4	43	46	7
	1990	0	4	40	49	7
	1993	1	2	46	48	3
Self-Managing Work Teams	1987	0	0	41	50	9
	1990	1	0	39	44	16
	1993	1	0	47	39	13
Minibusiness Units	1987	0	4	39	48	9
	1990	0	0	47	45	9
	1993	0	2	33	47	18
Employee Committees Concerned with Policy and/or Strategy	1987			— —not asked— —		
	1990			— —not asked— —		
	1993	2	1	42	50	6

approaches to employee involvement. This result may help explain why they are being implemented by more companies and suggests that their use will continue to increase.

The approaches rated in Table 9.2 drew a high percentage of undecided ratings, which may reflect the newness of these programs. It may also reflect the difficulty of installing and using them since they do require significant organizational changes.

The high success ratings given to all the employee involvement programs that emphasize power sharing are quite impressive. There are obviously a large number of satisfied users. This is especially significant given the newness of some of the practices and the fact that as technologies they are not well developed. Once they are better developed and understood, they may well be seen as even more effective.

Results of Employee Involvement Efforts

The overwhelming majority of companies believe that their overall employee involvement efforts are successful. This complements the findings reported in Sections 8 and 9, which show that specific practices are successful. As Table 10.1 indicates, fully 81 percent indicate that their experience has been positive or very positive, whereas only 1 percent of companies report a negative experience. The rest (18 percent) are neutral in their assessment.

Organizational effectiveness can be measured in two ways: changes in internal operating processes and changes in operating results. Table 10.2 looks at the first of these. It presents the results of a question that asked to what extent employee involvement activities have resulted in a series of improvements in important internal operating processes and business conditions.

There is considerable variation in the degree to which these internal operations have improved. The greatest improvement is reported in four areas: participatory management, trust, management decision making, and organizational processes and procedures.

Table 10.1	Overall, How Positive Has Your Experience Been with Your Employee Involvement Efforts?[1]
Very Negative	0%
Negative	1%
Neither Negative nor Positive	18%
Positive	68%
Very Positive	13%
[1]Percent of companies	

Table 10.2
Percentage Indicating at Least Some Improvement in Internal Business Conditions as a Result of Employee Involvement.

INTERNAL BUSINESS CONDITIONS	PERCENTAGE SAYING IMPROVED AT LEAST SOME[1]		
	1987 (N=323)	1990 (N=313)	1993 (N=279)
Increased Employee Trust in Management	79	66	73
Improved Organizational Processes and Procedures	76	75	82
Improved Management Decision Making	74	69	76
Improved Implementation of Technology	66	60	64
Improved Employee Safety/Health	55	48	60
Improved Union-Management Relations	43	47	46
Eliminated Layers of Management or Supervision	38	50	54
Changed Management Style to One That Is More Participatory	79	78	83

[1] Responded 2, 3, 4, or 5 on a 5-point scale: 1 = little or no extent; 5 = very great extent; "no basis to judge" also a possible response.

The result is generally consistent with arguments made in favor of employee involvement. These gains also fit with the type of employee involvement activities most frequently implemented—parallel problem solving. The most common outcome of parallel activities is suggestions on how to improve operations and decision making. Parallel processes also can be used to select new technologies and to make recommendations about their implementation. When the suggestions are listened to and acted upon they can increase trust in management. The results also fit with the implementation of TQM, since they can lead to improvements in operations.

The 1993 results are generally consistent with those found in 1987 and 1990. There is a slight overall tendency for the 1993 results to be more positive than the earlier ones, but the change is not a large one.

The most interesting change from 1987 to 1993 is an increase in the likelihood that layers of management will be eliminated. Eliminating layers of management is difficult to do and is not likely to result from parallel participation approaches. Substantial reduction does, however, tend to be associated with self-managing teams and minibusiness units (Lawler, 1992). As discussed earlier, these are being used with greater frequency. One outcome of the increased use of such practices may be a greater tendency for organizations to eliminate management layers. When EI activities involving teams and minibusiness units become more common and mature, they may produce further reductions in layers of management.

Table 10.3 gives information about perceived changes in performance results. The results reported by the respondents are grouped into three factors: direct performance outcomes, profitability and competitiveness, and employee satisfaction and quality of work life. As with the more global assessments of EI efforts, firms overwhelmingly report a positive experience for every outcome measured. Only for worker satisfaction (2 percent) and for employee quality of work life (1 percent) do any firms report a negative impact, and even here a clear majority of firms report positive results.

The responses indicate that companies perceive the strongest impact on direct performance outcomes, especially quality of prod-

Table 10.3	Perceived Impact of EI on Performance.						
	Mean*	Very Negative	Negative	Neither	Positive	Very Positive	No Basis to Judge
Direct Performance Outcomes							
Productivity	4.1	0	0	5	63	16	17
Quality of Product/Services	4.2	0	0	4	62	20	14
Customer Service	4.2	0	0	6	56	22	15
Speed of Response	4.0	0	0	10	59	13	18
Profitability and Competitiveness							
Competitiveness	3.9	0	0	14	57	7	22
Profitability	3.9	0	0	19	51	8	22
Employee Satisfaction and QWL							
Worker Satisfaction	4.0	0	2	13	59	12	15
Employee Quality of Work Life	3.9	0	1	15	58	7	19

* Mean score calculated with "no basis to judge" = missing.

ucts and services, customer service, and productivity. More than three-quarters of the sample report success in these areas. It is noteworthy that a relatively large number of respondents (more than a fifth of the sample) indicate that they are unable to judge the impact of employee involvement efforts on profitability and competitiveness, and a relatively large percentage also perceive no impact on these outcomes. Of those reporting either a positive or negative experience, however, most—two-thirds of respondents— rate it as positive.

The items listed in each factor cluster closely together, and the three types of outcomes also are interrelated. As Table 10.4 indicates, correlations among the three outcome factors are relatively high. Employee satisfaction and quality of work life are the most weakly linked to the other two types of outcomes. Direct performance outcomes are most closely related to profitability and competitiveness.

Table 10.5 provides detailed information on how the adoption of each employee involvement practice is related to each outcome measure, as well as to satisfaction with the overall EI effort. It is

Table 10.4 **Interrelationship of EI Outcomes.**

	Direct Performance Outcomes ✪	Profitability and Competitiveness	Employee Satisfaction and QWL
Direct Performance Outcomes ✪	—		
Profitability and Competitiveness	.52	—	
Employee Satisfaction and QWL	.42	.30	—
Satisfaction with EI Overall	.46	.42	.35

✪ (productivity, customer satisfaction, quality, and speed)

Note: All correlations are relatively strong and highly significant (p≤.001).

EI PRACTICE	Direct Performance Outcomes ✪	Profitability and Competitiveness	Employee Satisfaction and QWL	Satisfaction with EI Overall
Information (Index)	**.29***	**.27***	**.14***	**.23***
Corporation's Operating Results	.18**	.17*		.18**
Unit's Operating Results	.28***	.20**		.15*
New Technologies	.15*			.14*
Business Plans/Goals	.22***	.22***		.12*
Competitors' Performance	.25***	.28***	.13*	.28***
Knowledge (Index)	**.31***	**.31***	**.21****	**.31***
Group Decision-Making/ Problem-Solving Skills	.27***	.22***	.18**	.28***
Leadership Skills	.19**	.26***	.13*	.21***
Skills in Understanding the Business	.13*	.23***	.13*	.14*
Quality/Statistical Analysis Skills	.25***	.27***	.18**	.28***
Team-Building Skills	.19**	.21**		.26***
Job-Skills Training	.15*			.22***
Cross-Training	.29***	.16*	.16*	.18**
Rewards (Index)	**.17****	**.13***		**.24***
All-Salaried Pay Systems				
Knowledge/Skill-Based Pay		.15*		.16**
Profit Sharing	.17**	.20**		
Gainsharing				.18**
Individual Incentives		.14*		.18**
Work-Group/Team Incentives				.12*
Nonmonetary Recognition Awards	.14*			.26***
Employee Stock Ownership Plans	.13*			.19**
Flexible, Cafeteria-Style Benefits				
Employment Security	.17**	.26***	.20**	.21***
Open Pay Information		.19**		
Stock Option Plan				.12*
Power (Index)	**.22***	**.23***	**.23***	**.39***
Suggestion System	.20**			.22***
Survey Feedback				.25***
Job Enrichment or Redesign	.21***			.24***
Quality Circles				.23***
Employee Participation Groups	.24***			.29***
Union-Management QWL Committees				.17**
Minibusiness Units	.17*			.18**
Self-Managing Work Teams	.15*			.27***
Employee Policy/Strategy Committees	.25***			.27***

✪ (productivity, customer satisfaction, quality, and speed)

Significant correlation coefficients key:
     *   = weak but significant ($p \leq .05$)
   **   = moderate relationship ($p \leq .01$)
  ***   = strong relationship ($p \leq .001$)

interesting that the amount of training and information sharing are most closely related to direct performance outcomes, as well as to profitability and competitiveness. Use of reward practices is the most weakly linked to all four outcomes. Power-sharing practices are the most closely related to employee satisfaction and quality of work life and to general satisfaction with the EI effort. Although our index of power-sharing practices is relatively strongly tied to profitability and competitiveness as well as to employee satisfaction and QWL, no specific power-sharing practice is significantly related to either outcome measure.

The most important types of information for influencing outcomes appear to be information about the unit's operating results, business plans and goals, and competitors' performance. It is interesting that information about competitor performance is by far the strongest predictor of employee outcomes, as well as overall satisfaction with EI. Interestingly, in Section 2 we reported that it is the least frequently communicated type of business information. We suspect that information about competitors is often critical to gaining employee acceptance of the need for change. Such information may both make for a more effective change effort and engage employees constructively in efforts to confront the organization's environment.

Training has a significant impact on all EI outcomes. Training in group decision making and problem solving, leadership, skills in understanding the business, quality skills, and cross-training all appear to be relatively strong predictors of one or more outcomes.

Adoption of most of the reward practices is related to satisfaction with EI overall but is inconsistently related to direct performance outcomes and profitability and competitiveness. Profit sharing, knowledge- or skill-based pay, and open pay information are most strongly related to the company-oriented outcomes. The only reward practice that is tied to employee satisfaction and QWL is employment security. It is interesting that this practice is fairly strongly related to all four outcomes, a result consistent with the claim that security is necessary to facilitate the trust needed for successful EI efforts. Employment security helps ensure that employees will not lose their jobs as a result of contributing their ideas for organizational improvement.

Adoption of most power-sharing practices is related to direct performance outcomes, and all power-sharing practices are correlated with overall satisfaction with EI. The best predictors of performance outcomes are employee policy or strategy committees, employee participation groups, and job enrichment. The best predictors of overall satisfaction with EI are participation groups, self-managing teams, policy or strategy committees, and survey feedback. We are surprised to find that no individual power-sharing practices are related to profitability and competitiveness or employee outcomes, given the many claims in the literature for a link between these practices and organizational performance.

Table 10.6 indicates how different EI types result in different outcomes. As might be expected, the Low Involvement companies experience the least positive results for all four outcomes. There is no clear advantage for any of the other types, however. Job Involvement shows a slight advantage in profitability and competitiveness, while Business Involvement firms have a slight edge on employee outcomes and overall satisfaction with EI. All four types of firms, however, report a very positive experience with their EI efforts on all four outcomes.

It is clear that companies that use EI practices overwhelmingly believe that they receive significant benefits from them. The use of a wide variety of specific power-sharing, reward, information-sharing, and training practices is linked to specific positive impacts. Not even one practice is negatively related to any outcome. Clearly there is consistency in the perception of benefits from EI. In Section 13,

Table 10.6	Average EI Outcome Scores for EI Types.			
EI TYPE	Direct Performance Outcomes ✪	Profitability and Competitiveness	Employee Satisfaction and QWL	Satisfaction with EI Overall
Low Involvement	3.9	3.6	3.7	3.7
Suggestion Involvement	4.2	4.0	4.0	4.0
Job Involvement	4.3	4.3	4.0	4.0
Business Involvement	4.2	4.0	4.2	4.1
Other Involvement	4.2	4.0	3.9	4.0

✪ (productivity, customer satisfaction, quality, and speed)

Note: all outcomes are measured on a 5-point response scale.

we will address the question of whether there is evidence from financial measures of performance to support these perceptions.

SECTION 11

Results of TQM Efforts

A very high percentage (83 percent) of those companies with TQM programs report that their experience with them has been positive or very positive (see Table 11.1). This finding is in contrast to press reports that many organizations are dissatisfied with their programs and are abandoning them. We see no evidence of this.

Table 11.2 shows the perceptions of TQM's impact on a number of outcomes. For each of these, at least two-thirds of the respondents report that the impact of TQM has been positive, with almost no companies feeling that there have been negative effects. A significant number of respondents did report that they could not judge outcomes, perhaps because it was too early to tell. Another small group felt that the impact of TQM is neutral on particular outcomes.

The outcomes in Table 11.2 are clustered into three groupings or factors. These factors are highly correlated with one another, as well as with the overall rating of satisfaction with TQM. The first factor reflects the work performance outcomes that can be directly impacted by employee behavior: productivity, quality of products and services, customer service, and speed of response to customers. The average impact is highest for these outcomes. The second factor contains overall company performance outcomes: profitability

Table 11.1	Overall, How Positive Has Your Experience Been with Total Quality Management?
Very Negative	0%
Negative	1%
Neither Negative nor Positive	16%
Positive	66%
Very Positive	17%

Table 11.2   Perceived Impact of TQM.

	Mean*	Very Negative	Negative	Neither	Positive	Very Positive	No Basis to Judge
Direct Performance Outcomes							
Productivity	4.0	0	1	11	66	14	9
Quality of Product/Services	4.2	0	0	3	69	20	7
Customer Service	4.2	0	0	3	70	20	8
Speed of Response	4.0	0	0	9	68	11	12
Profitability and Competitiveness							
Competitiveness	4.0	0	0	9	68	9	14
Profitability	3.9	0	0	19	53	10	17
Employee Satisfaction and QWL							
Worker Satisfaction	3.8	0	1	19	61	6	13
Employee Quality of Work Life	3.8	0	1	21	56	7	16

* Mean score calculated with "no basis to judge" = missing.

and competitiveness. The third factor consists of the employee outcomes: satisfaction and quality of work life. Although clearly in the positive range, companies are experiencing slightly less impact in these last two areas than in the direct work performance arena. The number of undecided (neutral or no basis to judge) responses in the categories of profitability, employee quality of work life, and employee satisfaction are relatively high.

Table 11.3 shows how the use of the various TQM practices relates to the three kinds of outcomes and to overall satisfaction with TQM. It also shows that TQM practices contribute differently to these outcomes. Overall satisfaction with the TQM program is strongly related to the use of core practices, to production-oriented practices, and to the two individual practices: cost-of-quality monitoring and collaboration with suppliers. Satisfaction is also related to every individual practice except the use of work cells. The results are not so consistent with respect to other TQM outcomes, however.

The use of core TQM practices is strongly related to direct work performance outcomes and to company performance. It is less strongly related to employee outcomes. Only three core practices (the use of quality improvement teams, direct exposure of employees to customers, and the use of cross-functional planning) relate to employee outcomes. Use of all the core practices except

Table 11.3 — Relationship of Outcomes to Extent of Adoption of TQM Practices.

	PERCEIVED TQM OUTCOMES			
	Direct Performance Outcomes ✪	Profitability and Competitiveness	Employee Satisfaction and QWL	Satisfaction with TQM Overall
Core Practices Overall	.31**	.35**	.25**	.39**
Quality Improvement Teams	.27**	.34**	.30**	.38**
Quality Councils	.19*			.32**
Cross-Functional Planning	.23**	.30**	.21*	.25**
Process Reengineering		.20*		.23**
Work Simplification	.23**	.27**		.31**
Customer Satisfaction Monitoring	.28**	.27**		.26**
Direct Employee Exposure to Customers	.24**	.25**	.20*	.30**
Production-Oriented Practices Overall	.23**	.27**		.31**
Self-Inspection	.20*	.24**		.22*
Statistical Control Method Used by Front-Line Employees	.23**	.25**		.30**
Just-in-Time Deliveries		.21*		.27**
Work Cells or Manufacturing Cells				
Other Practices				
Cost-of-Quality Monitoring		.22*		.25**
Collaboration with Suppliers in Quality Efforts		.21*		.25**
Percent Employees Involved	.27**	.29**	.23*	.37**

✪ (productivity, customer satisfaction, quality, and speed)

Significant correlation coefficients key:
  *   = moderate relationship (p ≤ .01)
  ** = strong relationship (p ≤ .001)

reengineering relates to the direct performance outcomes. All except quality councils relate to company performance, although the reengineering relationship is weaker than the others. Reengineering may be too new a phenomenon to have achieved the impacts that its proponents predict for it.

The use of production-oriented TQM practices is not strongly linked to direct and company outcomes and it is not significantly related to employee outcomes. Three practices are related to company outcomes and two to direct performance outcomes, but none of the individual production-oriented practices is related to employee outcomes. This finding provides more evidence that the use of these practices is not being accompanied by programs that give employees a stake in the company.

The use of the two individual TQM practices, cost-of-quality monitoring and collaboration with suppliers, are tied to company performance outcomes but not to employee outcomes or direct work outcomes. This result is not surprising, since these two practices are often implemented in a way that is oriented directly to the bottom line.

We also examined whether the percentage of employees covered by TQM efforts relates to the outcomes. The results displayed in the bottom line of Table 11.3 show that the three overall outcomes and the company's overall satisfaction with TQM are all higher when a greater percentage of employees are covered.

The general pattern of relationships shows that TQM is contributing to company outcomes, especially to direct performance outcomes. This finding is supported by the finding that the amount of coverage by TQM practices is strongly related to company performance. There is also a strong relationship between core and production-oriented practices and direct work performance outcomes. There are few significant relationships with employee outcomes; however, the more widely companies use TQM practices, the more positive their impact on employees overall. Generally, employees seem to be experiencing less positive impact from TQM than companies do.

SECTION 12

Results of Combining Employee Involvement and TQM Programs

We argued earlier that although both TQM and EI stress employee involvement as well as training and skills development, there are also some key differences between them. The TQM literature attends more to work process and customer outcomes. The employee involvement literature emphasizes design of the work and business units for fuller business involvement and employee motivation. In addition, employee involvement emphasizes making the employee a stakeholder in business performance. In practice, these two management approaches may contribute to organizational effectiveness in a complementary and reinforcing manner such that their individual impact is weakened by the absence of the other.

Table 12.1 shows the correlations between the use of TQM practices and the company's perceived outcomes from its EI activities.

Table 12.1 — Relationship of EI Outcomes to TQM Indices.

TQM INDICES	EI OUTCOMES		
	Direct Performance Outcomes ✪	Profitability and Competitiveness	Employee Satisfaction and QWL
Core TQM Practices	.28**	.27**	.15
Production-Oriented Practices	.39**	.26**	.29**

✪ (productivity, customer satisfaction, quality, and speed)

Significant correlation coefficients key:
   * = moderate relationship (p ≤ .01)
   ** = strong relationship (p ≤ .001)

The use of the core TQM practices is related to the performance and company outcomes of EI but not to the employee outcomes from EI. In contrast to this finding, the use of the production-oriented TQM practices relates to all three kinds of EI outcomes. The positive relationship with employee outcomes is particularly interesting because the use of the production-oriented practices did not relate at all to employee outcomes from TQM. Apparently the positive employee outcomes from the establishment of work cells and the training of employees in self-inspection and statistical process control are being experienced as employee involvement outcomes, not as TQM outcomes. Overall the results suggest that the more organizations use TQM practices, the more positive results they get from their EI efforts. This provides evidence for the close and complementary relationship of the two initiatives.

Table 12.2 shows that most of the indices of employee involvement are related to the TQM outcomes, especially to company outcomes. The development of knowledge and empowerment, two emphases that are shared by TQM and EI, are both related to the employee outcomes of TQM. Rewards, by contrast, are not related to the outcomes of TQM. Overall the results suggest that the more organizations use EI practices, the more likely they are to have successful TQM programs.

Tables 12.3 and 12.4 provide additional evidence of the intertwined impact of EI and TQM. Table 12.3 shows that some of

Table 12.2	**Relationship of TQM Outcomes to EI Indices.**

	TQM OUTCOMES			
EMPLOYEE INVOLVEMENT INDICES	Direct Performance Outcomes ✪	Profitability and Competitiveness	Employee Satisfaction and QWL	Satisfaction with TQM Overall
EI Overall	.21*	.29**	.19	.25**
Information	.20*	.20*	.13	.14
Knowledge and Skills	.17	.31**	.20*	.27**
Power Sharing	.22*	.33**	.25**	.23**
Rewards	.11	.10	.00	.10

✪ (productivity, customer satisfaction, quality, and speed)

Significant correlation coefficients key:
  * = moderate relationship (p ≤ .01)
  ** = strong relationship (p ≤ .001)

Table 12.3	**Relationship of Extent of Use of TQM Practices and TQM Outcomes with and Without the Effect of EI.**

		TQM OUTCOMES		
		Direct Performance Outcomes ✪	Profitability and Competitiveness	Employee Satisfaction and QWL
Core TQM Practices	Without EI	.25***	.26***	.19
	With EI	.31***	.35***	.25***
Production-Oriented Practices	Without EI	.17	.18	.05
	With EI	.23***	.27***	.11

✪ (productivity, customer satisfaction, quality, and speed)

Significant correlation coefficients key:
  * = weak but significant (p ≤ .05)
  ** = moderate relationship (p ≤ .01)
  *** = strong relationship (p ≤ .001)

Note: Without = partial correlations
With = zero order correlations

the relationship of TQM practices to TQM outcomes is actually the result of introducing EI practices. The partial correlations between the use of core and production-oriented practices and the TQM outcomes all go down when the effect of EI is eliminated. The relationship between the use of core practices and employee outcomes loses its statistical significance, indicating that it resulted from employee involvement. The relationships of production-oriented practices to direct work performance outcomes and company performance also become nonsignificant without the EI impact.

The findings with respect to the impact of TQM and EI are not unexpected: most TQM proponents advocate high levels of employee involvement as a part of their TQM efforts. However, the findings do make a very important point: the impact of TQM programs that do not also include EI practices will be less positive both for employee outcomes and for performance outcomes.

Table 12.4 shows the impact of the use of EI approaches on EI outcomes when the impact of core and production-oriented TQM practices is eliminated. Again we see most of the relationships declining and many of them losing their significance. Without TQM practices, the overall use of EI and the amount of information that is shared remain significantly related to direct performance and company outcomes. Knowledge and skills are weakly tied to company outcomes under the same conditions. Only power sharing is weakly related to employee outcomes when the impact of TQM is partialled out. Thus it appears that the use of TQM practices is an important part of successfully involving employees in processes that lead to improvements in organizational performance.

The findings presented in Section 7 showed that companies using the most advanced form of EI, business involvement, are the greatest users of most TQM practices. Table 12.5 demonstrates that these companies also experience the greatest amount of TQM impact in two areas: profitability and competitiveness (where job involvement companies are almost as high) and employee satisfaction and QWL. Companies employing job involvement approaches report slightly higher impact of TQM on direct work performance outcomes, although the differences between the suggestion, job, and business involvement companies are not statistically significant for this outcome. Probably because it makes the employee a stakeholder in company and work performance, business involvement seems to create the most positive employee outcomes from TQM programs.

Table 12.4

Relationship of Extent of Use of EI Practices to EI Outcomes with and Without the Effect of TQM.

		EI OUTCOMES		
		Direct Performance Outcomes ✪	Profitability and Competitiveness	Employee Satisfaction and QWL
EI Overall	Without TQM	.20**	.17*	.14
	With TQM	.33***	.28***	.22***
Information	Without TQM	.21**	.20**	.08
	With TQM	.29***	.27***	.14*
Knowledge and Skills	Without TQM	.13	.18*	.08
	With TQM	.31***	.31***	.21**
Power Sharing	Without TQM	.06	.10	.15*
	With TQM	.22***	.23***	.23***
Rewards	Without TQM	.12	.09	.08
	With TQM	.17**	.13	.12

✪ (productivity, customer satisfaction, quality, and speed)

Significant correlation coefficients key:
    * = weak but significant (p ≤ .05)
   ** = moderate relationship (p ≤ .01)
  *** = strong relationship (p ≤ .001)

Note: Without = partial correlations—controlling for TQM core and production-oriented practices.
     With = zero-order correlations.

Table 12.6 shows that the manner in which TQM and EI are implemented and managed relates to the employee outcomes that result from both. The employee outcomes from TQM are higher in companies where EI started first or simultaneously with TQM than when TQM started first. It seems that these companies are better able to create the conditions for the employee to be an

Table 12.5 Relationship of TQM Outcomes to EI Type.

EI TYPE	TQM OUTCOMES		
	Direct Performance Outcomes ✪	Profitability and Competitiveness	Employee Satisfaction and QWL
Low EI	3.93	3.71	3.65
Suggestion Involvement	4.16	4.00	3.87
Job Involvement	4.24	4.17	3.75
Business Involvement	4.15	4.25	4.00
Other	4.10	4.00	3.84

✪ (productivity, customer satisfaction, quality, and speed)

Note: means are reported.

Table 12.6 Relationship of TQM and EI Outcomes to When EI and TQM Started.

		EI Started First	Simultaneous	TQM Started First
Direct Performance Outcomes ✪	EI	4.15	4.19	4.16
	TQM	4.12	4.16	4.05
Profitability and Competitiveness	EI	3.97	3.99	3.84
	TQM	3.93	4.05	3.88
Employee Satisfaction and QWL	EI	4.06*	3.95	3.87
	TQM	3.86*	4.00*	3.70

✪ (productivity, customer satisfaction, quality, and speed)

Key: * = Significantly higher than the unstarred time relationship.   Note: means are presented and compared.

Table 12.7	Relationship of TQM Outcomes to How EI and TQM Are Managed.		

		Two Separate Programs	Coordinated	One Integrated Program
Direct Performance Outcomes ✪	EI	4.04	4.20	4.21
	TQM	4.02	4.09	4.14
Profitability and Competitiveness	EI	3.78	3.90	4.00*
	TQM	3.85	3.96	4.00
Employee Satisfaction and QWL	EI	3.92	3.98	3.96
	TQM	3.70	3.76	3.89*

✪ (productivity, customer satisfaction, quality, and speed)

Key: * = Significantly higher than the other forms of managing.

Note: means are presented and compared.

important stakeholder in performance improvement through TQM. Employee outcomes from EI are also highest if EI starts first. Direct performance and company outcomes do not significantly differ depending on which started first, although it is interesting that the ratings in these areas are generally the lowest for companies in which TQM started first.

The employee outcomes from TQM and the company outcomes from EI are highest when the two initiatives are managed in an integrated fashion (see Table 12.7). Coordination helps somewhat, but both employee and company outcomes are highest if the two are integrated parts of a single improvement effort.

Finally, Table 12.8 shows that direct performance outcomes from both TQM and EI and the company outcomes from EI are perceived to be highest when EI is seen as an important part of TQM rather than the reverse. This result no doubt reflects the task-oriented focus of TQM. For better or for worse, it is often easier to get management commitment to these efforts if they see that the focus is directly on task and process, rather than on ways to involve employees in the business.

In summary, the evidence presented in this section substantiates the close interrelationship and complementary nature of employee involvement and total quality management. Companies with more extensive forms of employee involvement also have a broader application of TQM practices and report higher TQM outcomes than companies with less employee involvement. The impact of TQM practices goes down when the effect of EI is eliminated and vice versa. There is a particularly close link between the use of production-oriented TQM practices and that of employee involvement approaches. The positive impact of production-oriented TQM practices disappears entirely if they are not used in a manner that is highly involving. Employee outcomes are highest if EI is started before TQM. Performance outcomes are highest if managers focus on TQM and see EI as part of it rather than the other way around. Finally, the highest impact is achieved if EI and TQM are managed as an integrated program.

Table 12.8		Relationship of How EI and TQM Are Perceived to EI and TQM Outcomes.	
		EI Is an Important Part of TQM	TQM Is an Important Part of EI
Direct Performance Outcomes ✪	EI	4.20**	3.98
	TQM	4.14**	3.95
Profitability and Competitiveness	EI	3.95**	3.73
	TQM	3.97	3.80
Employee Satisfaction and QWL	EI	3.96	3.90
	TQM	3.86	3.67

✪ (productivity, customer satisfaction, quality, and speed)

Key: * = weak but significant (p ≤ .05)
** = moderate relationship (p ≤ .01)
*** = strong relationship (p ≤ .001)

Note: means are presented and compared.

SECTION 13

Financial Effects of Employee Involvement and TQM

What is the effect of employee involvement and total quality management practices on the financial performance of companies that adopt these practices? The answer to this question is of critical importance to the future of both EI and TQM. Ultimately, in order to survive, they must show that they improve corporate performance. At this point in time, the available research does not provide a definitive answer to this question.

There is a large body of research on the performance effects of EI and to a lesser extent TQM. Most studies have examined the effects of specific EI and TQM practices on work groups, plants, offices, and production lines (see, for example, Golembiewski and Sun, 1990; Cotton et al., 1988). In general, such studies report some positive effects and few negative effects. The results, which are important and encouraging, are consistent with the managerial perceptions we found in this study, if not quite so positive. However, studies looking at a whole range of practices are rare. Moreover, most studies do not address the question of whether the effects are strong enough to influence company performance.

Some studies have examined the effects of EI and related practices on performance within specific industries. Researchers have examined the steel, auto, apparel, and other industries. For example, MacDuffie and Krafcik (1992) found that an index of ten involvement-oriented practices predicted productivity and quality in a study of most auto assembly plants worldwide. These studies use many different measures of involvement, often making it difficult to know how well the findings apply to different combinations of EI practices. The focus on single industries is an advantage in that it automatically controls for many industry-specific differences in financial performance, technology, and a host of other factors that otherwise make it difficult to establish a direct relationship between management practices and financial performance. At the same time, findings from studies in one industry may not be generalizable to other industries.

The few studies that have examined the effects of EI and TQM practices on performance at the firm level are limited but encouraging. Denison (1990) looked at thirty-four firms that had completed employee attitude surveys in at least part of their organization. He found that firms with more participative culture scores have a higher return on investment and return on sales over a period of five years after the survey. Similarly, Hansen and Wernerfelt (1989) found that a participative culture, as measured by employee surveys, is related to return on assets in sixty firms. Both of these studies used employee attitudes as measures of culture; they did not measure the use of EI and TQM practices. Huselid (in press) used a broad index of human resource practices that overlaps in part with our measures of EI and TQM practices. He found a significant relationship between these practices and return on assets.

We should not underestimate the difficulty of demonstrating a relationship between EI and TQM practices and firm performance. The typical company uses most of these practices with between 1 and 20 percent of its workforce, and there are virtually no firms that use them on an organization-wide basis. Thus it is impossible to compare truly high users with low users in order to see how much effect these practices have. The impacts of employee involvement and total quality management must therefore be strong for them to be detected in statistical analyses because there is limited variability in the amount firms use these approaches. In addition, the typical EI or TQM effort is only a few years old—most firms are still learning how best to implement and manage the use of these practices. Furthermore, their effects in many cases may only be starting to appear in the firms' financial results because it takes time for management practices to change behaviors and for behavioral changes to result in changes in financial results. Finally, how a firm is organized and managed is one of many influences on its financial performance.

In order to examine the effects of EI and TQM practices on firm financial performance measures, we obtained data on company performance in 1993 from Compact Disclosure, a database on thousands of companies. We were able to obtain data on 757 companies for the analyses that we report. This figure is less than the total number of companies in the Fortune 1000 for several reasons. Firms that were acquired or merged before the performance data were published were not included in the database. Also it does not provide complete coverage of Fortune 1000 firms, especially the smaller firms in the Service 500. The database covers some firms but does not necessarily provide data on all the measures we needed for our analyses. Finally, we also draw on the industry coding and data on company employment levels that are reported in *Fortune*.

We used two measures of firm economic productivity in 1993. The first is total factor productivity, a relatively sophisticated economic measure of the efficiency with which firms use capital and labor. The second is sales per employee, a simple but relatively common productivity indicator. We used four measures of financial return in 1993. These were return on sales, return on assets, return on investment, and total return to investors. Some consider return on sales and return on assets to be most closely related to corporate efficiency, whereas return on investment and total return to investors are indicators of overall corporate effectiveness. The latter obviously is of special interest to investors (it may, however, be affected by stock market trends).

Our statistical analyses used a number of control variables. There are strong industry effects for return measures and firm productivity. For example, sales per employee and return on investment tend to be systematically different for the steel and banking industries. Thus we controlled for industry in our analyses and were obliged to use performance data for all available firms, not just those that completed surveys in 1993. We constructed a control variable for firms that did not provide a survey. We also controlled for capital intensity—that is, property, plant, and equipment per employee. These can vary systematically both across and also within industries and can greatly influence performance on financial outcome measures. We considered using level of union membership as a control variable because one element of our power-sharing index is union-management QWL committees. However, inspection of the data indicated that controlling for union membership was not necessary and did not change the results.

We conducted a multiple regression analysis of the effects of EI and TQM on each performance outcome. We first trimmed the sample by eliminating the top and bottom 1 percent of firms on each measure. This is a common procedure in the analysis of firm performance; it recognizes that extremely good or extremely poor performance is more likely due to the market or other factors than to EI and TQM practices. We next entered all the control variables together in a block. Finally, we entered the EI indices for power sharing, information sharing, rewards, and training, as well as the TQM indices of core practices and production-oriented practices, in a block. This statistical technique recognizes that the EI and TQM scales are correlated. These correlations between the predictor measures make it impossible to disentangle the relative effects of specific practices or indices statistically, although it is possible to examine the combined effects of these practices.

This analysis is unique among the available studies. The predictors are our indices of EI and TQM practices, not a broader or narrower range of human resource practices. Our predictor measures look at the use of specific practices, not employee attitudes that may be due to their effects. The level of analysis is the company. Last, we use a number of different company-level performance measures as outcomes, not just one or two measures.

The control variables are strongly related to the six measures of performance. The controls account for a large portion of the variance in each case, confirming the importance of using them when analyses are done to determine the effects of management practices on firm performance.

The regression results reported in Table 13.1 indicate that overall use of EI and TQM practices is significantly related to six measures of corporate performance. The strength of the relationship varies. Sales per employee is marginally related to the use of EI and TQM

Table 13.1 — **Regression Results for Financial Results and Usage of EI and TQM.**

OUTCOME MEASURE	EI AND TQM VARIABLES Significance Level
Total Factor Productivity	*
Sales per Employee	+
Return on Sales	*
Return on Assets	**
Return on Investment	*
Return on Equity	***
Total Return to Investors	not significant

Key: + p ≤ .10
         * p ≤ .05
        ** p ≤ .01
       *** p ≤ .001
      **** p ≤ .0001

Note: all significance levels are one-tailed F tests.

practices, whereas return on equity is most strongly related to EI and TQM use. Given the limited use of EI and TQM practices by the typical firm in the sample and their relatively recent adoption, the discovery of any significant effects is important.

The finding of a significant relationship suggests that there may be a causal relationship between the adoption of management practices and firm performance. It, of course, does not prove causality because these are correlational not experimental results. There are a variety of alternative explanations for the relationships we have reported here. For example, it is possible that firms with higher rates of return adopt EI and TQM practices because they can afford to do so. Other factors may also explain both adoption and performance.

One way to rule out alternative explanations for the relationship between EI and TQM practices and financial performance is through the analysis of changes in practices and performance over time. Because of shifts in the makeup of the sample and the changing composition in the Fortune 1000, our sample of repeated firms is too small to enable us to do an adequate longitudinal matched-sample analysis from 1987 to 1993. Nevertheless, we can shed more light on causality by examining the lagged relationship of employee involvement to financial performance. This approach assumes, as we have argued, that the financial performance effects from the implementation of EI and TQM will not be observable for several years because of the time it takes for people to learn how to perform effectively in these new ways and to introduce improvements in processes and methods.

Table 13.2 shows a summary of the results of regression analyses using the 1987 EI index score to predict average financial performance in the period from 1989–1991 (these analyses are described in greater detail in Levine, Ledford, Lawler, and Mohrman, 1995). A three-year average for firm performance was used to reduce the impact of anomalies such as large write-offs that may result in nonrepresentative one-year performance data. This time period is the only one reported because the financial data required to perform the same analyses for 1990 and 1993 EI data were not available at the time of the writing of this book. Unfortunately no quality data were collected in 1987 so we can only investigate EI effects.

Five of the seven performance measures during the 1989–1991 period were significantly related to the levels of adoption of EI practices in 1987. As with the 1993 cross-sectional data, total return to investors is not significantly related to EI, nor is sales per employee. The close similarity of these lagged results to the cross-sectional results reported in Table 13.1 is impressive. Despite the fact that the samples of companies were not identical, different years were used, and lagged years of data were used, significant relationships exist. This finding lends support to the belief that a significant part of the relationship between employee involvement and performance is due to the adoption of the practices causing performance rather than the reverse.

How large is the effect of EI and TQM on corporate performance? Statistically the percentage of the performance variance that is accounted for by EI and TQM practices is relatively small. Even so,

Table 13.2	Regression Results for 1989–1991 Financial Results and 1987 EI Usage.

	EI AND TQM VARIABLES
1989–1991 OUTCOME MEASURE	1987 EI Practice Significance Level
Total Factor Productivity	*
Sales per Employee	not significant
Return on Sales	*
Return on Assets	**
Return on Investment	*
Return on Equity	*
Total Return to Investors	not significant

Key:
+ $p \leq .10$
* $p \leq .05$
** $p \leq .01$
*** $p \leq .001$
**** $p \leq .0001$

Note: all significance levels are one-tailed F tests.

Source: Levine, Ledford, Lawler, and Mohrman, 1995.

because of the wide range of corporate performance, a small movement in the use of EI and TQM practices can translate into a relatively large effect on financial performance.

One way to estimate how much a change in one variable will cause another to change is to look at the effect of a one standard deviation change in the variable. A one standard deviation increase in the use of EI and TQM practices means covering approximately an additional 30 percent of employees. This is a large increase that represents at least a doubling of many companies' present EI and TQM efforts, but it is achievable as is shown by the significant number of companies already at this level.

A one standard deviation increase has quite noticeable effects on five of the performance measures. Only the effect on sales per employee is negligible. An increase in coverage is associated with increases in total factor productivity of 1.0 percent; return on assets, 1.1 percent; return on sales, 2.0 percent; return on investment, 2.8 percent; and return on equity, 3.1 percent.

Table 13.3 compares the financial performance of high, medium, and low adopters of EI and TQM practices. It presents the results for firms at the mean, those one standard deviation above the mean, and those one standard deviation below the mean in use of EI and TQM practices. These are differences that should capture the attention of anyone concerned with firm performance since they suggest that millions of dollars in additional performance is realized by companies that are above average in the adoption of EI and TQM practices.

Table 13.3	Financial Effect of EI and TQM Usage.		
FINANCIAL MEASURES	Low Use	Medium Use	High Use
Return on Sales	6.3	8.3	10.3
Return on Assets	4.7	5.8	6.9
Return on Investment	9.0	11.8	14.6
Return on Equity	16.6	19.7	22.8

We believe the relationship between employee involvement, total quality management, and firm performance is intriguing and significant. It suggests that firms can improve their financial performance by adopting an appropriate mix of EI and TQM practices. This idea supports the very favorable ratings we received when firms were asked to rate the success of their EI and TQM programs and practices. Overall our study suggests that EI and TQM work and that the firms adopting them can gain a significant competitive advantage.

PART FOUR

Who Adopts Employee Involvement and TQM Programs?

Coverage of Employee Involvement and TQM Practices

Companies report greater coverage with TQM than with EI programs for each of nine different occupational groupings (see Table 14.1). Manufacturing employees are the most extensively covered by both EI and TQM. Seventy-six percent of companies report using TQM with about half or more of their manufacturing employees. The application of TQM is almost as high for customer-service employees, first-level management, and top-level management (thus, especially high use of TQM exists with employees involved in manufacturing, those who serve the customer directly, and those who manage them). Fifty-three percent of companies report covering about half or more of their manufacturing employees with EI. About the same percentage of top management is covered.

Sales and marketing are the least likely to be covered by either TQM or EI. Fifty-three percent of companies report using EI with fewer than 40 percent of their sales and marketing employees. EI coverage is almost as low for distribution and for engineering, technical, and scientific employees. Forty-four percent of companies use TQM with fewer than 40 percent of their sales and marketing personnel. The lower coverage of sales and marketing employees may reflect the isolation of these two groups of employees from the rest of the organization. In some companies, the commission structure for sales employees makes it difficult to deflect their attention from selling activities to organizational improvement activities, and to involve them in cross-functional activities. In addition, in many technical firms, marketing employees tend to be marginalized, and it is difficult to integrate their activities with those of the technical and manufacturing segments of the company.

The greater overall usage of TQM reflected in these data provides clear evidence that in some companies these practices are being used without employee involvement efforts. The implementation of TQM without EI is not advisable since, as the results of this study show, it is less effective and does not lead employees to feel that they are being treated as serious organizational stakeholders.

Tables 14.2 and 14.3 illustrate the relationship between amount of coverage and the outcomes for EI and TQM respectively. Degree of manufacturing-employee coverage by both TQM and EI is

Table 14.1 — Coverage of Different Occupational Groupings: EI and TQM.

What percentage of employees who perform each of the following kinds of work are covered?

	Type	Mean*	None (0%)	Almost None (1–20%)	Some (21–40%)	About Half (41–60%)	Most (61–80%)	Almost All (81–99%)	All (100%)
Manufacturing	EI	4.4	8	9	21	10	18	22	13
	TQM	4.9	8	8	8	9	20	25	22
Customer Service	EI	4.2	4	16	24	10	19	14	13
	TQM	4.7	3	14	16	8	18	17	23
Distribution	EI	3.8	8	22	22	12	13	14	10
	TQM	4.5	6	17	13	11	14	19	21
Sales and Marketing	EI	3.8	5	26	22	12	12	13	10
	TQM	4.2	5	22	17	13	9	11	22
Engineering/ Technical/ Scientific	EI	3.9	5	23	23	14	12	12	11
	TQM	4.4	5	15	16	16	13	13	22
Staff Support (e.g., information systems, human resources, etc.)	EI	4.0	5	20	22	12	15	14	12
	TQM	4.4	4	19	14	14	15	12	23
First-Level Management	EI	4.1	3	19	23	12	16	15	12
	TQM	4.7	1	13	16	13	19	15	24
Middle Management	EI	4.2	3	21	18	12	16	18	12
	TQM	4.6	2	17	14	16	14	16	23
Top Management	EI	4.4	6	23	14	4	12	18	24
	TQM	4.7	4	22	11	5	12	14	32

*Mean = scale of 1–7.

Table 14.2 **Relationship of EI Coverage to EI Outcomes.**

PERCENT COVERED	Direct Performance Outcomes ✪	Profitability and Competitiveness	Employee Satisfaction and QWL
Manufacturing	**		*
Customer Service	**	**	
Distribution	*	**	*
Sales and Marketing	*	**	
Engineering/Technical/Scientific	*	*	
Staff Support (e.g., information systems, human resources)	*	**	
First-Level Management	*	**	*
Middle Management		**	
Top Management			

✪ (productivity, customer satisfaction, quality, and speed)

Significant correlation coefficients key:
     *   =   moderate relationship (p ≤ .01)
    **   =   strong relationship (p ≤ .001)

related to the direct performance outcomes, but only EI manufacturing coverage is related to employee satisfaction and quality of work life. Surprisingly the degree of manufacturing employee coverage is not related to profitability and competitiveness.

A striking but not unexpected pattern is the very strong relationship of management coverage by TQM to all outcomes. Having management involved is clearly a high payoff activity. It is frequently argued that the involvement of management is critical in ensuring that TQM activities are effectively directed at strategically important issues. It also is needed to make sure that processes can be changed to improve work outcomes and that employees develop a stake in these activities.

Table 14.3	Relationship of TQM Coverage to TQM Outcomes.		

PERCENT COVERED	Direct Performance Outcomes ✪	Profitability and Competitiveness	Employee Satisfaction and QWL
Manufacturing	*		
Customer Service	**	*	**
Distribution	**	*	**
Sales and Marketing	**	*	**
Engineering/Technical/Scientific	**		
Staff Support (e.g., information systems, human resources)	**	*	**
First-Level Management	**	**	**
Middle Management	**	**	**
Top Management	**	**	*

✪ (productivity, customer satisfaction, quality, and speed)

Significant correlation coefficients key:
    *   = moderate relationship ($p \leq .01$)
    ** = strong relationship ($p \leq .001$)

First-level management coverage by EI is related to all three types of EI outcomes. This result underscores the key role of first-level management in changing the management practices of the company and in enabling the line employee to become more highly involved in improving performance. An unexpected finding is that top-management EI coverage is not related to any outcomes, and middle-management EI coverage is linked only to the company outcomes.

In general, degree of coverage with TQM practices has a greater impact on direct performance outcomes and on employee satisfaction than does degree of coverage with EI practices. This finding probably reflects the direct focus of TQM on work processes. By contrast, EI coverage of the various occupational groupings is highly related to company outcomes, profitability, and competitiveness—consistent with its emphasis on business involvement and organizational design. The lack of statistically significant relationships between EI and employee outcomes is puzzling, given the emphasis of employee involvement on the motivational aspects of organization. It may indicate that a highly involving organization requires a level of commitment, job demands, and even stress and uncertainty that offsets the benefits of participation and empowerment.

Engineering/technical/scientific employees are the group whose degree of coverage with both EI and TQM is least related to outcomes. These employees often already have high levels of job autonomy. Furthermore, many companies have had a more difficult challenge attaining meaningful business and process improvement involvement in these work areas.

Overall, the results concerning coverage reinforce the conclusions drawn earlier. EI provides a general focus on improving the business, as well as the motivational and organizational design focus to tie employee interest to business outcomes. TQM offers a particular set of tools for influencing work processes and performance. Together they constitute a more effective approach to organizational improvement than if either is used separately. The results also show that amount of coverage is an important determinant of TQM and EI success—the more employees in all functions and at all levels are covered, the better the outcome.

SECTION 15

Organizational Size, Downsizing, and Delayering

The results of the 1987 and 1990 surveys indicated that larger firms are significantly more likely than smaller ones to adopt most EI practices. This was not a surprising finding. Organizational size, as measured by number of employees, has been found to be one of the best predictors of innovation adoption in general (Rogers, 1983). Larger firms tend to have greater resources for innovation, including corporate staff groups to champion change and provide change-oriented support. In addition, larger organizations are more complex and diverse, factors that can increase the number of places where innovation can be initiated.

Organizational Size. Larger firms may have a greater need for both EI and TQM. They often experience motivational problems because it is hard for employees and managers to see the impact of their work on the customer and on company performance. Large size also can lead to employees feeling part of an impersonal, bureaucratic system. Moreover, the work in large firms is more likely to be highly segmented, with many different groups being involved in complex processes and with many places where work-process problems can result from hand-offs and conflicting priorities. Employees in large firms are therefore prime targets for the kinds of process-improvement changes that are part of TQM programs.

Nevertheless, several factors work against the successful establishment and dissemination of innovation in large organizations. First, segmentation, bureaucratic structure, and resulting rigidity all can interfere with the ability of the organization to develop a common approach to change or to disseminate successful innovation throughout. In addition, size makes it hard for large-scale change initiatives to have a quick impact on company performance. Managers may become discouraged with the pace of change, and employees may have difficulty believing that the initiatives are serious or that they can make a difference. Furthermore, most large companies have a history of change initiatives that are experienced as the "flavor of the month"; they are championed by different parts of the organization and are not coordinated. The result can be that employees ignore or resist change efforts.

Table 15.1 shows the significant relationship between organization size and the adoption of employee involvement practices. It indicates that larger firms continue to have greater adoption of EI practices than smaller firms, although the differences are not nearly so sweeping as they were in 1987 and 1990. In general, larger firms tend to make more use of employee involvement overall and of power-sharing and reward-sharing practices in particular. These relationships have been constant over the three time periods with the exception of 1987, when the use of reward practices was not related to size.

In 1993, the use of three involvement practices is significantly related to size. Larger firms make more use of survey feedback, a technique widely employed to sense attitudes and climate. Large firms also make greater use of knowledge- and skill-based pay and employment security agreements. The relationship between size and skill-based pay is especially interesting because it is a practice that was *not* more likely to be used by larger firms in past surveys. Apparently much of the increase in skill-based pay is occurring in larger firms, perhaps in part to provide job-growth and career-growth paths in their new downsized and delayered structures.

Although large companies continue to use employee involvement and in particular power and reward practices more than smaller

Table 15.1	**Firm Size and Employee Involvement (EI) Practices.**[1]		

EMPLOYEE INVOLVEMENT	1987	1990	1993
EI Overall	✔	✔	✔
Information Overall			
Unit Operating Results	✔	✔	
Business Plans/Goals		✔	
Competitors' Performance		✔	
Knowledge and Skills Overall			
Group Decision-Making/Problem-Solving Skills		✔	
Leadership		✔	
Team Building	✔	✔	
Job Skills		✔	
Rewards Overall		✔	✔
Gainsharing		✔	
Nonmonetary Recognition Awards		✔	
Employee Stock Ownership Plans		✔	
Knowledge/Skill-Based Pay			✔
All-Salaried Workforce	✔(-)		
Employment Security			✔
Power Sharing Overall	✔	✔	✔
Survey Feedback	✔	✔	✔
Job Enrichment/Redesign	✔	✔	
Quality Circles	✔	✔	
Employee Participation Groups Other Than Quality Circles	✔	✔	
Union-Management Quality of Work Life (QWL) Committees	✔	✔	
Self-Managing Work Teams	✔	✔	

All correlations are positive unless noted with (-). Only significant relationships are shown.

[1] Firm size is significantly correlated ($p \le .05$).

companies, the relationship is weakening. In 1987 and 1990, larger companies were more likely to use all but one of the power-sharing practices. In 1990, the use of a number of information, knowledge, and reward practices was also related to size. In 1993, use of only three practices is related to size. It appears that with these exceptions smaller companies are catching up with larger companies. Coverage of these practices in the popular press may be partially responsible for drawing the attention of smaller companies to them.

Table 15.2 shows the significant relationships between size and the use of TQM practices for 1990 and 1993, the only two years for which the TQM questions were asked. In 1990, the use of five of the six TQM practices was significantly related to organizational size. By 1993, only one practice, the use of just-in-time deliveries, was related to size. Again, larger companies appear to have been the early adopters, but smaller companies are catching up.

Table 15.3 shows that in the 1993 results, larger companies do not experience greater outcomes as a result of their use of EI or TQM. In 1987 and 1990, only a few of the internal conditions were more likely to be positively affected in larger firms. Although larger companies were apparently the early adopters, smaller companies seem to have experienced as great an impact. In part, this may be because the larger companies served as the learning grounds for the development of these approaches; as a result, smaller companies were able to accelerate their implementation and avoid mistakes. In addition, the finding may reflect the extremely difficult and time-consuming nature of change in larger companies.

Downsizing and Delayering. During the past decade, companies took many measures to strengthen their competitive position. Downsizing and delayering are two of the most prominent. In some cases they led the change: companies cut levels and head count and then expected the remaining organizational members to find new ways to do things with fewer people. This approach sometimes led "through the back door" to changes in processes and to increased

Table 15.2	Firm Size and Total Quality Management (TQM) Practices.[1]		
TOTAL QUALITY MANAGEMENT		1990	1993
Core Practices Overall			
Direct Employee Exposure to Customers		✔	
Work Simplification		✔	
Production-Oriented Practices Overall			
Self-Inspection		✔	
Just-in-Time Deliveries		✔	✔
Work Cells or Manufacturing Cells		✔	
Percentage Covered by TQM		✔	

[1] Firm size is significantly and positively correlated (p ≤ .05). Only significant relationships are shown.

Table 15.3	Firm Size and Effects of EI and TQM Involvement.		
	1987	1990	1993
Performance Impact of EI	No relationship	No relationship	No relationship
Changes in Internal Business Conditions as a Result of EI	Union-management relations[1]	Union-management relations[1] Moving decision making lower[1] Employee safety and health[1]	No relationship
Performance Impact of TQM	Not asked	Not asked	No relationship

[1] Firm size is significantly correlated.

involvement and the empowerment of people. In other cases, downsizing and delayering were the result of a planned reconfiguration of work processes. Employee involvement was encouraged by moving managerial responsibilities and decision making closer to the location at which products were developed and manufactured and services delivered.

In 1993, 47 percent of the firms studied reported that they decreased in size during the past ten years (see Table 15.4), while 48 percent reported growing in size. Thus these firms show a high level of change in size, but they have not necessarily become smaller. This may not have been the experience of all firms during the period; here the focus is on the "winners" who are in the Fortune 1000. As is shown in Table 15.5, 72 percent of firms have eliminated at least one layer in the past ten years, with 60 percent of those having reduced two or more levels. Many of these firms have therefore eliminated layers of management even though they have not necessarily downsized.

There has been considerable debate about whether a move toward employee involvement is possible in an environment characterized by downsizing and delayering. These activities result in greater job insecurity and perhaps less commitment as employees lose the sense that the company will provide a job for them as long as they carry out their responsibilities. In addition, downsizing may

Table 15.4	Changes in Size of Workforce in Last Ten Years.

Approximately how much has the size of your workforce changed in the last ten years?

	1993
Decreased by More Than 50%	5.1%
Decreased 41 to 50%	6.3%
Decreased 31 to 40%	7.4%
Decreased 21 to 30%	9.2%
Decreased 10 to 20%	10.7%
Decreased Less Than 10%	8.8%
No Change	4.8%
Increased Less Than 20%	10.7%
Increased 21 to 40%	10.3%
Increased 41 to 60%	3.7%
Increased 61 to 80%	2.6%
Increased 81 to 100%	3.7%
Increased More Than 100%	16.9%

cause increased stress as a result of work overload and insecurity. At the same time, reduction in layers of management can result in more autonomy and responsibility for line employees and fewer required approvals. Delayering can result in swifter decision making and more ownership over decisions. In fact, in many organizations it is difficult to imagine creating meaningful employee involvement unless the size and shape of the control-oriented hierarchy are changed.

| Table 15.5 | Number of Layers of Management Removed During Last Ten Years. |

NUMBER OF LAYERS REMOVED	Percent of Companies That Have Delayered
One	40.2%
Two	45.5%
Three	9.0%
Four	3.7%
Five	1.1%
Six or more	0.5%

Table 15.6 shows the relationship of downsizing and removing layers to the use of employee involvement practices in 1990 and 1993 (the downsizing and delayering questions were not asked in 1987). In 1993, the main area in which firms that have downsized differ from those that have not is in their use of reward practices. Downsized organizations are more likely to have employed team or work-group incentives but *less* likely to have profit sharing or stock option plans for their employees. Not surprisingly, they also are less likely to have employment security policies.

This pattern of reward practices is interesting because it suggests that downsizing companies are trying to use pay to stimulate increased performance in parts of the organization. However, these firms are not so likely to link employees to the overall financial viability of the firm. They are also not more likely to have built the other conditions for employee involvement in business success by sharing information, developing skills, or sharing power. In these areas, these companies clearly are not purposefully adapting to their new size by creating a high-involvement organization. The only exception is that downsized firms are more likely to utilize union-management committees. Much of the same pattern existed in 1990; there were no areas in which there were significant differences in the use of EI practices by downsized firms.

Table 15.6

Relationship of Downsizing and Removing Layers to Use of Employee Involvement Practices.[1]

	COMPARED TO THOSE THAT HAVE NOT			
	Firms That Have Downsized (N=130)		Firms That Have Removed Layers (N=128)	
EI PRACTICES	1990	1993	1990	1993
EI Overall				more use
Information Overall				more use
Information About Unit's Operating Results				more use
Information on Business Plans/Goals				more use
Knowledge and Skills Overall				
Group Decision-Making/ Problem-Solving Skills				more use
Team-Building Skills				more use
Rewards Overall				
Gainsharing			more use	
Skill-Based Pay			more use	
Profit Sharing		less use		
Work-Group or Team Incentives		more use		
Employment Security		less use		
Stock Option Plan		less use		
Nonmonetary Recognition Awards				more use
Power Sharing Overall				more use
Union-Management QWL Committees		more use	more use	more use
Survey Feedback				more use
Job Enrichment or Redesign				more use
Minibusiness Units			more use	more use
Self-Managing Work Teams				more use
Employee Committees Concerned with Policy and/or Strategy				more use

[1] All relationships are significant (p ≤ .05).

A very different pattern of EI and TQM adoption differentiates firms that have reduced management layers from those that have not. Here we see greater use of employee involvement practices overall, particularly of information sharing and power sharing. Since 1990, there has been considerable growth in the number of areas of EI adoption where delayered organizations exceed those that have not delayered. Thus it appears that flattening the organization drives or accompanies the introduction of involvement practices in a way that is not true if the organization simply downsizes. It underscores the perspective that creating a highly involving organization requires a redesign of an organization's structure. The only area where there is not greater adoption by delayered firms is in the area of rewards. Interestingly this is a change from 1990, when delayered firms were more likely to use gainsharing and skill-based pay.

Table 15.7 shows that the use of TQM practices was not related to downsizing or delayering in 1993; there was only a relationship to the percentage of employees involved in the TQM program. In 1990, firms that removed layers and downsized were more likely to use several of the production-oriented approaches and to monitor the cost of quality. The 1993 finding that delayering does not seem to be associated with the use of TQM is a marked difference from the pattern for the use of EI. This outcome probably reflects the greater emphasis of EI on pushing decision making down and restructuring.

In 1993, delayered firms felt that EI practices have a greater impact on internal organizational conditions (see Table 15.8). Delayered

| Table 15.7 | Relationship of Downsizing and Removing Layers to Use of TQM Practices.[1] |

| | COMPARED TO THOSE THAT HAVE NOT | | | |
| | Firms That Have Downsized | | Firms That Have Removed Layers | |
TQM PRACTICES	1990	1993	1990	1993
Core Practices Overall	no significant differences			
Production-Oriented Practices Overall				
Just-in-Time Deliveries			more use	
Work Cells or Manufacturing Cells	more use		more use	
Other Practices				
Cost-of-Quality Monitoring	more use		more use	
Percent Employees Involved		greater		lower

[1] All relationships are significant ($p \leq .05$).

Table 15.8

Relationship of Downsizing and Removing Layers to Impact and Outcomes of Employee Involvement Practices.[1]

	COMPARED TO THOSE THAT HAVE NOT			
	Firms That Have Downsized (N=130)		Firms That Have Removed Layers (N=128)	
EI PRACTICES	1990	1993	1990	1993
Organizational Impact				
Improved Implementation of Technology				greater impact
Eliminated Layers of Management or Supervision		greater impact		not applicable
Changed Management Style to One That Is More Participatory			greater impact	greater impact
Improved Union-Management Relations		greater impact	greater impact	greater impact
Moved Decision-Making Authority to Lower Organizational Levels			greater impact	greater impact
Moved Performance-Based Rewards to Lower Organizational Levels				greater impact
Broadened Skill Development at Lower Organizational Levels			greater impact	greater impact
Increased Information Flow Throughout Corporation				greater impact
Increased Employee Trust in Management				greater impact
Improved Management Decision Making				greater impact
Improved Employee Safety/Health				
Improved Organizational Processes and Procedures		greater impact	greater impact	greater impact
Increased Speed of Decision Making				greater impact
Improved Implementation of Decisions				greater impact
Employee Involvement Outcomes				
Direct Performance Outcomes (productivity, customer satisfaction, quality, and speed)		greater impact		
Profitability and Competitiveness				
Employee Satisfaction and QWL				

[1] All relationships are significant (p ≤ .05).

companies reported more impact in almost every area than those that had not delayered. This trend was also present to a lesser degree in the 1990 data.

In 1993, companies that had reduced their size were more likely to have eliminated layers of management, improved union-management relations, and improved organizational processes and procedures as a consequence of their EI initiatives. In 1990, there was no difference between downsized organizations and those that had grown or stayed the same in the extent to which they felt EI was changing internal conditions.

There is only one difference in the perceived organizational outcomes of EI in companies that have downsized and delayered compared to those that have not. Companies that have downsized report greater impact of EI on the direct work-performance outcomes. Although companies that reduce layers use more EI approaches and see a greater impact on internal conditions, this action apparently does not translate into a greater impact on performance outcomes.

Analyses of the relationship between downsizing and delayering and the impact of TQM practices show nothing significant. With respect to TQM, downsizing and delayering are thus not associated with the use of these practices or with their impact.

Overall, downsizing does not seem to have a major effect on the implementation and impact of EI and TQM practice. By contrast, delayering has a positive impact on both. It is associated not only with greater adoption of EI practices but also with their producing positive results.

SECTION 16

Differences Between Service and Manufacturing Organizations

The 1987 and 1990 surveys found that service companies use employee involvement practices less extensively than do manufacturing firms. This result is not surprising since the genesis of many practices is in manufacturing settings, where phenomena such as new design plants (Lawler, 1978), sociotechnically designed work units (Pasmore, 1988), quality circles, and many TQM practices have demonstrated the viability of involvement.

In 1993, manufacturing firms also outpaced service companies in their adoption of many aspects of EI and TQM, although service firms seem to be selectively applying certain practices at a higher rate. Table 16.1 shows the EI areas in which service or manufacturing firms are highest for each survey. Manufacturing firms continue to be higher in EI overall and in the use of knowledge and skills training and power sharing. In the area of skills development,

Table 16.1 — Service/Manufacturing Differences in EI Use.[1]

SERVICE FIRMS USE MORE				MANUFACTURING FIRMS USE MORE		
1987	1990	1993		1987	1990	1993
			EI Overall		✔	✔
			Information Overall		✔	
			Competitors' Performance		✔	
		✔	Advance Information on New Technologies That May Affect Them			
			Unit Operating Results	✔	✔	
			Knowledge and Skills Overall		✔	✔
			Group Decision-Making/Problem-Solving Skills		✔	✔
			Team Building		✔	
			Quality/Statistical Analysis Skills	✔	✔	✔
✔			Business Skills			
			Rewards Overall		✔	
✔	✔	✔	All-Salaried Pay Systems			
			Gainsharing		✔	✔
			Skill-Based Pay		✔	
✔	✔	✔	Flexible, Cafeteria-Style Benefits			
		✔	Open Pay Information			
			Power Sharing Overall		✔	✔
			Quality Circles	✔	✔	
			Employee Participation Groups Other Than Quality Circles	✔	✔	✔
			Union-Management QWL Committees	✔	✔	✔
			Minibusiness Units		✔	✔
			Self-Managing Work Teams	✔	✔	✔

[1] Differences are significant (p ≤ .05).

manufacturing concerns in particular lead in the amount of training in group problem solving and quality and statistical analysis tools. In 1990, they used team building more extensively as well.

Manufacturing firms also continue to lead in the use of almost all power-sharing practices: participation groups other than quality circles, union/management QWL committees, self-managing teams, and minibusiness units. In earlier years, they also had more extensive use of quality circles. Their greater utilization of these practices may reflect the earlier start of many manufacturing firms. Service firms may catch up as they gradually train and involve more people.

In 1993, manufacturing and service firms reported about equal rates of sharing information, except that service firms were more likely to share information about new technologies that affect the workforce. This is probably a response to the large investment that the service sector has been making in information technology, which involves significantly upgraded skills and the dislocation of many workers (Mills, 1991; Schneider and Bowen, 1995). Manufacturing was more likely to share unit results and information about competition in the 1990 survey, but those differences did not exist in 1993.

Service firms covered the workforce more extensively with three reward practices in 1993: all-salaried workforce, open sharing of pay information, and flexible cafeteria-style benefits. Service firms are significantly less likely to be unionized, and the all-salaried and flexible benefits approaches may be more achievable in a non-union environment. In 1990, manufacturing firms made more use of reward practices, especially gainsharing and skill-based pay. In 1993, the difference in the application of skill-based pay disappeared. Manufacturing firms are still more likely to use gainsharing, a difference that may reflect the difficulty that many service firms are experiencing in defining formulas that link service jobs to financial performance.

Table 16.2 shows the proportion of service and manufacturing firms in each of the EI types. Over half of the service firms report having low EI in the majority of their operations; this figure

Table 16.2	Relative Proportion of Service and Manufacturing Firms in Different EI Types.	
	Manufacturing Firms	Service Firms
Low EI	30.0%	52.2%
Suggestion Involvement	48.5%	26.5%
Job Involvement	6.9%	5.3%
Business Involvement	6.2%	7.1%
Other	8.5%	8.8%

compares with 30 percent of the manufacturing firms. This pattern is reversed, however, for suggestion involvement, with almost half of manufacturing firms participating, compared to only 26.5 percent of service firms. About the same percentage of service and manufacturing companies are in the job involvement and business involvement categories. The service firms that use significant employee involvement are more likely to redesign work and try to establish business involvement than are manufacturing firms. Again this result is consistent with earlier patterns suggesting that much EI and TQM in manufacturing settings is undertaken without developing a true business partnership.

Table 16.3 compares the use of various kinds of TQM practices by manufacturing and service firms. As indicated by their name, all of the production-oriented practices are used more extensively by manufacturing companies. This is also true of cost-of-quality monitoring and collaboration with suppliers. These differences are steady since 1990. Yet there are no differences on most of the core TQM practices. Service firms are more likely to employ customer satisfaction monitoring and direct employee exposure to customers. Customer satisfaction is a natural measure for those firms whose workers are exposed to customers as a integral part of their work; thus it can be anticipated that service firms are higher in

Table 16.3	**Service/Manufacturing Differences in TQM Practices.**[1]			
SERVICE FIRMS USE MORE			MANUFACTURING FIRMS USE MORE	
1990	1993		1990	1993
not asked		**Core Practices**	not asked	
not asked	✔	Customer Satisfaction Monitoring	not asked	
✔	✔	Direct Employee Exposure to Customers		
not asked		**Production-Oriented Practices**	not asked	✔
		Statistical Control Method Used by Front-Line Employees		✔
		Self-Inspection	✔	✔
		Just-in-Time Deliveries	✔	✔
		Work Cells or Manufacturing Cells	✔	✔
		Other Practices		
		Cost-of-Quality Monitoring	✔	✔
		Collaboration with Suppliers in Quality Efforts	✔	✔

[1] Differences are significant (p ≤ .05).

these areas (Bowen and Lawler, 1992). What is surprising is the finding that service firms are as high as manufacturing companies on the other core practices, including the use of quality improvement teams and councils, reengineering, cross-functional planning, and work simplification. This shows a significant commitment to TQM in the service industry.

Table 16.4 shows the relative percentages of service and manufacturing companies with different levels of TQM coverage. Thirty-nine percent of service and only 11.5 percent of manufacturing firms have no TQM coverage. However, 27 percent of manufacturing firms and 22 percent of service firms cover all employees. A substantial portion of both service and manufacturing companies therefore have a company wide commitment to TQM. What distinguishes service and manufacturing firms is that the latter are more likely to use TQM in parts of their operations.

A comparison of the impact of EI and TQM in service and manufacturing firms yields a mixed picture. Table 16.5 shows that employee involvement initiatives have had a larger impact on internal organizational conditions in manufacturing than in service firms. This outcome may reflect long-term usage as well as the more extensive training and creation of power-sharing mechanisms that are characteristic of manufacturing firms. Although the differences

Table 16.4	Relative Proportion of Service and Manufacturing Firms with Different Amounts of TQM Coverage.	
PERCENT COVERED	Manufacturing Firms	Service Firms
0	11.5%	38.8%
1–25	16.2%	14.8%
26–50	11.6%	14.0%
51–75	13.6%	5.0%
76–99	19.6%	4.9%
100	27.7%	22.3%

Table 16.5

Table 16.5 — Service/Manufacturing Differences in Impact and Outcomes of EI Efforts[1]

HIGHER IMPACT IN SERVICE FIRMS				HIGHER IMPACT IN MANUFACTURING FIRMS		
1987	1990	1993		1987	1990	1993
			Internal Business Conditions			
			Eliminated Layers of Management or Supervision		✔	✔
			Improved Union-Management Relations		✔	✔
			Moved Decision-Making Authority to Lower Organizational Level		✔	✔
			Increased Employee Trust in Management		✔	✔
			Improved Management Decision Making		✔	✔
			Improved Employee Safety/Health		✔	✔
			Improved Implementation of Technology		✔	
			Initiated More Participative Management Style		✔	
			Broadened Skill Development		✔	
			Increased Information Flow		✔	
			Improved Organizational Processes/Procedures		✔	
			Performance Results			
			DIRECT PERFORMANCE OUTCOMES		✔	
✔			Productivity		✔	✔
✔			Quality of Products or Services		✔	✔
			PROFITABILITY AND COMPETITIVENESS		✔	
			EMPLOYEE SATISFACTION AND QWL		✔	✔
			Worker Satisfaction		✔	

[1] Only differences significant at $p \leq .05$ are shown.

are not as across the board as they were in 1990, manufacturing firms still report that they have done more to eliminate layers of management, move decision making lower, and increase trust and quality of decision making. In addition, union-management relations have improved to a greater extent, as have health and safety.

Table 16.5 also shows that manufacturing firms report they have experienced a greater impact on productivity and quality as well as on employee outcomes as a result of their employee involvement efforts. These differences in perceived outcomes between manufacturing and service companies have been increasing since 1987. In 1993, there were no differences in the impact on company profitability and competitiveness.

There were also no differences between service and manufacturing firms in any of the outcomes they reported as a result of their

TQM efforts. This may reflect the pattern of adoption shown earlier. Even though a smaller percentage of service firms have a TQM initiative, those that do are on average as heavily invested in it as manufacturing firms. Thus it is not surprising that those that have it are getting comparable results.

The overall picture with respect to service and manufacturing is that service firms do not apply employee involvement practices so extensively as manufacturing firms. This is particularly true for suggestion-oriented approaches. Service firms are just as likely to employ business and job involvement approaches. Furthermore, although a much greater percentage of service firms have no TQM initiative at all, a substantial number have an extensive commitment to TQM. Service firms are less likely to use production-oriented TQM; however, they are just as likely to use the core approaches to it. Manufacturing firms were the early adopters of EI and still report a greater impact on internal business conditions, productivity and quality, and employee outcomes. There is no difference between service and manufacturing in reported TQM outcomes.

SECTION 17

The Impact of Competitive Environment

The increased global competition that many U.S. companies face has been well documented. The impact of the competition has been felt in some business sectors for over a decade, thus there is good reason to believe it may have had a significant effect on how some organizations are managed. One possible response to competitive pressures is to adopt employee involvement and total quality practices in order to gain the advantages they offer. In the 1990 and 1993 surveys, we asked questions about the competitive conditions that companies confront. In this section, we investigate the relationship between competitive market conditions and the adoption of employee involvement and total quality management practices.

Table 17.1 presents data on the kinds of competitive market conditions companies face. At least two-thirds of the companies report experiencing the following market conditions to some extent: foreign competition, shorter product-life cycles, declining markets, rapid growth, intense cost competition, rapid change, and speed-to-market competition. Intense cost competition stands out as the most commonly experienced condition. There is no evidence to show that the environment changed significantly from 1990 to 1993.

Table 17.2 shows that three conditions are strongly related to the adoption of employee involvement practices: foreign competition,

| Table 17.1 | **Characteristics of Competitive Business Environment.** |

To what extent is your corporation's business environment characterized by the following conditions?

		Mean	Little or No Extent	Some Extent	Moderate Extent	Great Extent	Very Great Extent
Subject to Heavy Foreign Competition	1990	2.5	37	21	14	17	11
	1993	2.4	32	27	15	18	9
Rapidly Growing Market	1990	2.2	33	32	23	9	4
	1993	2.2	35	32	19	12	3
Shorter Product-Life Cycles	1990	2.4	33	22	26	14	6
	1993	2.5	29	24	22	20	6
Declining Markets	1990	2.2	30	38	19	10	4
	1993	2.4	22	35	27	12	5
Intense Quality Competition	1993	3.6	3	14	27	36	21
Intense Speed-to-Market Competition	1993	3.4	10	13	24	33	20
Intense Cost Competition	1993	4.4	0	2	10	32	56
Rapid Change	1993	3.9	1	10	24	32	32

Note: 1990 data included when available.

rapidly growing markets, and extreme performance pressures. The most powerful of the three appears to be extreme performance pressures. This measure was created by combining the responses to a series of statistically related questions indicating that an organization has to perform at very high levels in order to compete effectively. The items included rapid environmental change, intense cost competition, powerful speed-to-market competition, shorter product-life

EI PRACTICES	Foreign Competition	Extreme Performance Pressures ✪	Declining Markets	Rapidly Growing Markets
EI Overall	*	***		***
Information Overall				*
Overall Operating Results	*			
Unit Operating Results	**			
New Technologies				*
Business Plans/Goals				
Competitors' Performance				*
Knowledge Overall	*	***		***
Group Problem Solving	**	*		
Leadership				***
Business Understanding		*		***
Quality/Statistical/Analysis	***	**		**
Team Building	*	**		*
Job-Skills Training		**		
Cross-Training		*		
Rewards Overall		***		***
All-Salaried Workforce				
Skill-Based Pay				***
Profit Sharing		***		***
Gainsharing				
Individual Incentives		***		***
Work-Group or Team Incentives		***		
Nonmonetary Recognition Awards for Performance	*	***		**
Employee Stock Ownership				
Flexible, Cafeteria-Style Benefits		*		
Employment Security				
Open Pay Information			*	
Stock Option Plan		**		***
Power Sharing Overall	***	***		
Job Redesign	*	***		
Quality Circles	***	*		
Participation Groups	**	*		
Union-Management QWL Committees	**	*		*
Minibusiness Units	*	**		*
Self-Managing Teams	***	***		**
Suggestion System				
Survey Feedback		*		*
Employee Committees Concerned with Policy/Strategy		**		

✪ Rapid change, intense cost competition, intense speed-to-market competition, shorter product-life cycles, and intense quality competition.

Key: * = weak but significant (p ≤. 05)
        ** = moderate relationship (p ≤.01)
       *** = strong relationship (p ≤. 001)

cycles, and intense quality competition. When companies face an extremely difficult competitive environment, employee involvement apparently becomes an attractive strategy; the reason undoubtedly is that it promises significant improvements in organizational performance rather than just the incremental change that might come about as a result of perfecting an existing management approach.

There is also a strong relationship between rapidly growing markets and the adoption of employee involvement practices. This result is somewhat unexpected since our analysis of the 1990 survey data did not find this strong relationship. Perhaps in the interim, organizations have increasingly decided to use employee involvement as a way of adapting to the demands that growth places on an organization.

The amount of foreign competition is also related to the adoption of some employee involvement practices, particularly those involving power sharing. This result follows logically from the consistent relationship between performance pressure and the adoption of employee involvement. Foreign competition usually is difficult competition. Furthermore, adoption may be helped by the publicity that problem-solving groups and other participative practices have gained as a result of their implementation in Japan.

Decline in markets appears to make very little difference in the adoption of employee involvement, probably because a decline in markets makes it difficult to justify transition costs. Moreover, EI may not be seen as a solution to the cost reductions that often need to be made in a declining situation.

The results concerned with adoption of total quality management practices are presented in Table 17.3. They are very similar to the results for the adoption of employee involvement, with one consistent exception. Rapidly growing markets tend not to have as strong a relationship to the adoption of total quality management practices. Foreign competition and extreme performance pressures are clearly related to their implementation.

Overall the results suggest that both TQM and employee involvement are likely to be adopted when an organization faces tough competitive pressure. This finding supports the arguments that they are perceived to be effective in improving performance and that they can often be complementary.

The results presented in Table 17.4 indicate that the more companies experience increased foreign competition and extreme busi-

TQM PRACTICES	Foreign Competition	Extreme Performance Pressures ✪	Declining Markets	Rapidly Growing Markets
Core Practices Overall	*	*		
Quality Improvement Teams	**	*		
Quality Councils		*		
Cross-Functional Planning	**	**		
Process Reengineering	*			
Work Simplification	*			
Customer Satisfaction Monitoring				
Direct Employee Exposure to Customers				
Production-Oriented Practices Overall	***	***		*
Self-Inspection	*	**		
Statistical Control Method Used by Front-Line Employees	***	*		
Just-in-Time Deliveries	**	***		**
Work Cells or Manufacturing Cells	***	**		*
Other Practices				
Cost-of-Quality Monitoring	*	*		*
Collaboration with Suppliers in Quality Efforts	*	*		

✪ Rapid change, intense cost competition, intense speed-to-market competition, shorter product-life cycles, and intense quality competition.

Key: * = weak but significant (p ≤ .05)
     ** = moderate relationship (p ≤ .01)
    *** = strong relationship (p ≤ .001)

ness pressures, the more likely they are to feel that their employee involvement practices have a positive impact on their internal business conditions. This result adds further support to the conclusion that employee involvement tends to be a frequent and effective response to increased foreign competition and extreme performance pressures. There is a particularly strong relationship between companies experiencing these conditions and their moving decision-making authority to lower organizational levels. Extreme performance pressure is also strongly associated with investing in the skills of lower-level employees, improved management decision making, increased speed of decision making, and improved organizational processes procedures.

Table 17.4 also reports results with respect to the effect of market conditions on the performance impact of employee involvement. There is relatively little relationship between the degree to which organizations experience foreign competition and extreme performance

	Foreign Competition	Extreme Performance Pressures ✪	Declining Markets	Rapidly Growing Markets
Internal Business Conditions				
Improved Implementation of Technology	*			
Eliminated Layers of Management or Supervision	*			
Changed Management Style to One That Is More Participatory		*		
Improved Union-Management Relations	***	*		
Moved Decision-Making Authority to Lower Organizational Level	***	**		
Broadened Skill Development at Lower Organizational Levels		**		
Increased Employee Trust in Management		*		
Improved Management Decision Making		***		
Improved Employee Safety/Health	*			
Improved Organizational Processes and Procedures		*		
Increased Speed of Decision Making		**		**
Improved Implementation of Decisions		**		
Performance Results				
DIRECT PERFORMANCE OUTCOMES				
Productivity	*	*		
PROFITABILITY AND COMPETITIVENESS				
EMPLOYEE SATISFACTION AND QWL	**			
Worker Satisfaction	*			
Employee Quality of Work Life	**			

✪ Rapid change, intense cost competition, intense speed-to-market competition, shorter product-life cycles, and intense quality competition.

Key: * = weak but significant (p ≤ .05)
       ** = moderate relationship (p ≤ .01)
       *** = strong relationship (p ≤ .001)

[1] Only significant relationships are shown.

pressures and their evaluation of the impact of their employee involvement programs. This is not the same finding that was obtained in the 1990 survey. There a strong relationship was found, particularly in the case of foreign competition. Organizations that faced foreign competition reported greater performance improvement as a result of adopting employee involvement.

There is no obvious reason for the change from 1990 to 1993. The finding from the 1990 survey fits the argument that employee involvement is particularly likely to pay off when the market requires performance improvement. The failure of this same finding to appear in the 1993 data is unexpected and raises the question of whether employee involvement can work well regardless of the amount of competitive pressures found in the external environment.

An analysis of the relationship between market conditions and the impact of TQM practices on organizational performance showed no significant relationships. Organizations that face more competitive business conditions did not report more positive impacts of their TQM programs. Although somewhat surprising, this result is generally consistent with the weak relationships found between market conditions and the impact of employee involvement on performance.

Overall market conditions seem more likely to influence the adoption of TQM and employee involvement practices than to influence how successful they are in contributing to organizational performance. Presumably their success is a function of the factors already considered in earlier parts of this book, as well as how well they are installed and whether they fit the situation in which they are being tried. The lack of a strong relationship does not mean that the practices do not have a positive impact on organizational performance. As indicated earlier, they do; it simply means that their effect is not necessarily more favorable when market conditions are highly competitive. This finding, of course, leads to the conclusion that they can have a positive impact regardless of the type of market condition an organization faces.

SECTION 18

The Influence of Union Status

The role of unions in employee involvement efforts has been the subject of intense debate. Somewhat less attention has been given to the role of unions in TQM programs. The backdrop for this debate is the steady decline of union membership in U.S. corporations. Today less than 12 percent of the private sector workforce belongs to a union, versus more than one-third of the workforce at the high-water mark just a few decades ago. The debate has engaged those within the labor movement (for example, AFL-CIO, 1985; Parker and Slaughter, 1988, Bluestone and Bluestone, 1993), as well as outside observers (for example, Hoerr, 1991; Kochan and Osterman, 1994; Cohen-Rosenthal, 1995). Some union leaders fear that employee involvement is just another way for management to manipulate workers and undermine unions, whereas others hope that joint management employee involvement efforts will bring benefits to unions members, bring credit to union leaders, and help bring about more constructive union-management relationships. Finally, some argue that employee involvement will have the greatest success when unions support them.

On the management side, some managers see unions as a major obstacle to their EI and TQM efforts. Others support the idea that it is important to have unions as partners in an EI or TQM effort; without them, there is a limit on the changes that can be made and there is no one to represent the workforce in decision making.

The intensity of discussion about these issues has not impeded unions from engaging in some employee involvement efforts. Virtually every major national union has been involved in a significant union-management employee involvement program. The United Auto Workers, the United Steelworkers of America, and the Communications Workers of America have been particularly active. Therefore the question is not whether unions can be engaged in EI and TQM efforts, but rather what forms these efforts take and what results they achieve.

Figure 18.1 examines the level of union involvement in EI efforts in firms that have at least part of their workforce unionized. The results indicate that in general unions are only somewhat involved in these efforts. Unions are seen as greatly or very greatly involved in only 19 percent of companies with unions. The overall pattern of involvement has hardly changed from 1987 to 1993.

The small amount of union involvement in EI efforts is disturbing. It suggests that in many situations union leaders are not influencing these activities. This situation creates the potential for conflict between management and unions over employee involvement efforts. In the absence of union involvement, there are also distinct limits to the scope of employee involvement activities. Pay systems, job classifications, work rules, and other important issues are collective-bargaining matters. They cannot be legally addressed without the unions. There is the additional danger that unions may be undermined by employee involvement efforts that do not include them (Bluestone and Bluestone, 1993).

It is surprising and disappointing that the level of union involvement in EI efforts has not changed. Clearly management has increased its support for these efforts. Why haven't unions? There are at least three possible reasons. First, unions see EI as a threat because it makes them unnecessary. Second, union leaders may

To what extent, if at all, are unions involved in employee involvement efforts?[1]

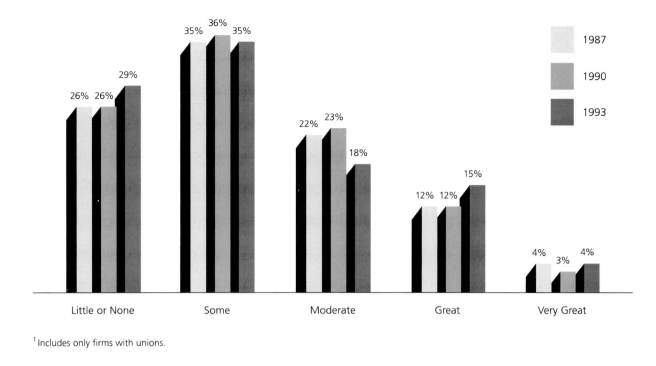

¹ Includes only firms with unions.

Figure 18.1. Union Involvement in EI Efforts.

find the changes it requires to be difficult and uncomfortable. Third, management may not welcome union involvement, and as a result unions are limited in what they can do.

Figure 18.2 presents the results concerning the extent of union involvement in TQM efforts. The results are very similar to those for EI. Since the question was asked only in 1993, it is impossible to determine if change has occurred, but it seems reasonable to assume that it has not.

How does unionization affect the types of employee involvement practices that are used? Table 18.1 indicates the practices most frequently employed in firms with unions and in those without them. There are some differences in the use of various information, knowledge, and power-sharing practices that are related to degree of unionization. Companies without unions are more likely to share information, to offer training in how to understand the business, and to cross-train employees. Rewards innovations are also

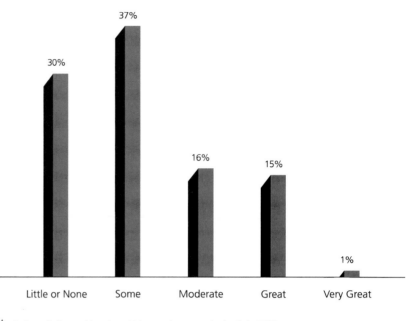

To what extent, if at all, are unions involved in Total Quality Management efforts?[1]

37%

30%

16%

15%

1%

Little or None   Some   Moderate   Great   Very Great

[1]Includes only firms with unions. This question was asked only in 1993.

Figure 18.2. Union Involvement in TQM Efforts.

related to unionization. Unionized firms are less likely to use an all-salaried workforce, profit sharing, and flexible benefits but are more likely to use gainsharing.

In order to determine if the percentage of the workforce that is unionized has an effect, we analyzed the data separately for firms with unions. For these companies, we correlated percentage of union membership with the adoption of EI practices. The result showed nothing of significance. Overall the results are similar to those found in 1987 and in 1990: firms with unions are slightly less likely to use most EI practices with the exception of union-management QWL committees.

Table 18.2 shows that unionized organizations are somewhat more likely to use two TQM practices: quality circles and quality councils. One explanation for this finding is that in many unionized firms these have become the major employee involvement and quality improvement practices because they are acceptable to unions.

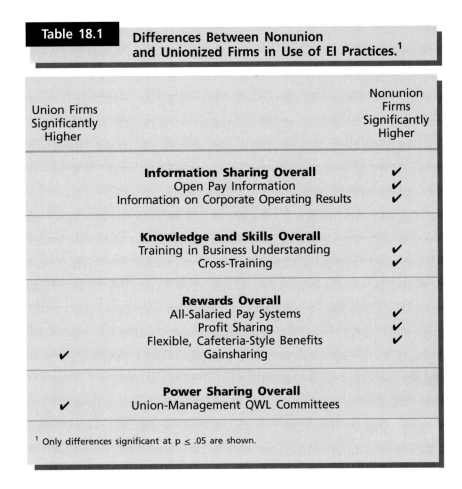

Table 18.1   Differences Between Nonunion and Unionized Firms in Use of EI Practices.[1]

Union Firms Significantly Higher		Nonunion Firms Significantly Higher
	Information Sharing Overall	✔
	Open Pay Information	✔
	Information on Corporate Operating Results	✔
	Knowledge and Skills Overall	
	Training in Business Understanding	✔
	Cross-Training	✔
	Rewards Overall	
	All-Salaried Pay Systems	✔
	Profit Sharing	✔
	Flexible, Cafeteria-Style Benefits	✔
✔	Gainsharing	
	Power Sharing Overall	
✔	Union-Management QWL Committees	

[1] Only differences significant at $p \leq .05$ are shown.

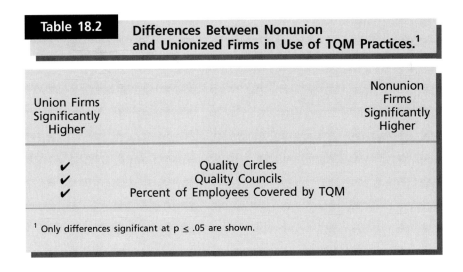

Table 18.2   Differences Between Nonunion and Unionized Firms in Use of TQM Practices.[1]

Union Firms Significantly Higher		Nonunion Firms Significantly Higher
✔	Quality Circles	
✔	Quality Councils	
✔	Percent of Employees Covered by TQM	

[1] Only differences significant at $p \leq .05$ are shown.

Looking only at firms with unions, we correlated the percentage of employees in unions with the adoption of TQM practices. The results were somewhat unanticipated. The adoption of most TQM practices was negatively related to the percentage of the workforce in unions. In other words, the more unions represent the entire workforce of an organization, the less likely it is to adopt TQM practices.

In general, the presence of a union is not related to the impact on performance of employee involvement efforts. There is a positive relationship only between the presence of a union and the impact of employee involvement efforts on employee health and safety, an important focus of most unions. It is significant that the degree of unionization had no negative effects on the impact of EI on any performance area or on any change in internal business conditions. Therefore the belief of some managers that unions are a barrier to effective employee involvement efforts is not supported by our data.

In order to better understand the effects of unions, we did one further analysis. For firms in which at least some employees belong to a union, we looked at the relationship between degree of union involvement and effects of employee involvement efforts. These data are presented in Table 18.3. Degree of union involvement was related to virtually every measure of performance and competitiveness.

Table 18.3	**Degree of Union Involvement and Effects of EI.**

Degree of union involvement in EI initiatives is significantly correlated (p ≤ .05) with the following:

Performance Results	Direct Performance Outcomes Overall
	   Quality
	   Speed of response
	   Customer service
	
	Profitability and Competitiveness Overall
	   Competitiveness
	
	Quality of Work Life

Changes in Internal Business Conditions	Improved Implementation of Technology Changed Management Style Improved Union-Management Relations Moved Decision Making to Lower Organizational Levels Moved Performance-Based Rewards to Lower Organizational Levels Broadened Skill Development at Lower Organizational Levels Increased Information Flow Throughout Corporation Increased Employee Trust in Management Improved Management Decision Making Improved Employee Safety/Health Improved Organizational Processes/Procedures Increased Speed of Decision Making Improved Implementation of Decisions

As was true in 1990, degree of union involvement is also related to every internal business condition except elimination of top-management layers. Degree of union involvement is strongly related to improved implementation of new technology, change to a more participative management style, better union-management relations, greater decision making at lower levels of the organization, movement of performance-based rewards to lower levels, broadened skill development at lower levels of the organization, increased information flow, increased employee trust in management, improved management decision making, improved employee safety and health, and improved organizational processes and procedures.

Table 18.4 presents data on the relationship between union involvement in TQM and the effects of TQM practices. Degree of union involvement is positively related to performance outcomes, competitiveness, and quality of work life.

The very consistent pattern of the relationships between union involvement and the success of EI and TQM efforts supports the argument that in unionized firms unions should participate in organizational improvement efforts. Without their involvement, the activities are much less likely to be successful.

Table 18.4	Degree of Union Involvement and Effects of TQM.

Degree of union involvement in TQM initiatives is significantly, positively correlated with the following:

Performance Impact	Direct Performance Outcomes Overall Productivity Quality Customer service
	Competitiveness
	Quality of Work Life

PART FIVE

The Future of Employee Involvement and TQM

SECTION 19

Plans for Adopting Employee Involvement and TQM

A series of questions in the survey addressed the future utilization of employee involvement and total quality management practices. Figure 19.1 offers data showing that employee involvement spending is likely to increase between 1993 and 1996. Most organizations report that they plan either to hold constant their spending on employee involvement activities or to increase it. Particularly significant is that only 6 percent of the organizations surveyed plan to decrease their spending, whereas 57 percent plan to increase it.

The 1987 responses indicated that spending was likely to increase, and our data suggest that it did. The 1990 responses indicated a somewhat larger increase was planned, and our results suggest that spending did grow. The increase projected in the current data is

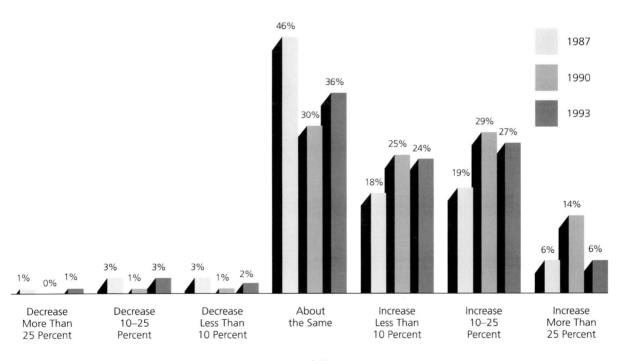

Figure 19.1. Percentage Change in Employee Involvement Spending in Next Fiscal Year.

slightly less than the one in the 1990 study, but this is not surprising. Increases of the size projected in 1990 simply cannot continue no matter how successful the activities. At some point, large increases on top of large increases cannot be justified from a cost perspective; ultimately they reach a ceiling when the total organization is covered by EI practices. Overall, employee involvement is likely to continue to be in a growth mode. This finding is consistent with the generally positive picture concerning the fit of employee involvement with the strategic plans of organizations and the results of employee involvement efforts so far.

Areas of Projected Growth. Table 19.1 takes the issue of future plans one step further by reporting data on the types of suggestion involvement activities likely to see increased use in the next two years. As can be seen, employee participation groups and survey feedback activities are projected for the greatest increases, results

| Table 19.1 | Percentage Planning Adoption/Discontinuation of Suggestion Involvement Practices. |

		Completely Discontinue	Decrease Use	Stay the Same	Increase Use	Greatly Increase Use
Quality Circles	1990	5	11	57	21	6
	1993	7	9	67	16	2
Employee Participation Groups Other Than QCs	1990	1	0	27	57	15
	1993	1	0	26	64	10
Union-Management QWL Committees	1990	5	3	68	22	2
	1993	3	2	71	20	4
Survey Feedback	1990	1	1	44	47	7
	1993	0	0	38	51	10
Suggestion Systems	1990			— —not asked— —		
	1993	2	7	48	37	6

consistent with our findings in 1990. Once again quality circles are not expected to show a large increase. They clearly appear to have topped out in popularity.

Table 19.2 presents the results for work-redesign approaches. Self-managing work teams and job enrichment show the highest level of projected increase, as they did in 1990. The 1990 predictions turned out to be accurate, so there is every reason to believe that more power will be moved to the lower levels of organizations.

Self-managing work teams appear to be on a particularly fast growth track. As noted earlier, a comparison among the 1987, 1990, and 1993 data shows a dramatic increase in the degree to which organizations utilize these teams. Self-managing work teams obviously became much more popular in the time period from 1987 to 1993, and there is every indication that they will become more so. There are a number of things that can account for their popularity, including their perceived positive results and the extensive amount of publicity that they have received in national magazines and other publications.

Table 19.2	Percentage Planning Adoption/Discontinuation of Work-Redesign Involvement Practices.					
		Completely Discontinue	Decrease Use	Stay the Same	Increase Use	Greatly Increase Use
Job Enrichment or Redesign	1990	1	2	38	57	3
	1993	1	0	35	57	6
Self-Managing Work Teams	1990	3	0	37	53	7
	1993	1	0	31	58	10
Minibusiness Units	1990	6	1	71	21	1
	1993	3	1	67	27	2
Employee Committees Concerned with Policy and/or Strategy	1990	— — not asked — —				
	1993	2	1	52	41	4

The three other practices expected to increase the most—survey feedback, job enrichment, and participation groups—are ones that already have a very high adoption rate. Their increased use would be particularly significant because it could lead to their affecting a majority of individuals in the firms that adopt them. This situation should create more total employee involvement organizations in contrast to companies where involvement is practiced in parts.

Table 19.3 presents the results for employee involvement–oriented reward systems. Some highly utilized reward-system practices are expected to see greater use; knowledge- or skill-based pay plans are projected to grow by 50 percent of the companies answering the questionnaire. This projection fits with the expected increase in the utilization of self-managing work teams since they often go together. Similar growth was projected in 1990, and in fact an increase did occur.

| Table 19.3 | Percentage Planning Adoption/Discontinuation of EI-Supportive Reward Practices. |

		Completely Discontinue	Decrease Use	Stay the Same	Increase Use	Greatly Increase Use
All-Salaried Pay Systems	1990	1	3	75	20	1
	1993	1	7	78	12	1
Knowledge/Skill-Based Pay	1990	2	0	45	49	4
	1993	1	2	47	45	5
Flexible, Cafeteria-Style Benefits	1990	1	1	47	44	8
	1993	0	1	58	34	7
Employment Security	1990			——not asked——		
	1993	4	9	82	4	1
Open Pay Information	1990			——not asked——		
	1993	3	1	75	17	4

Only one practice—employment security—is expected to decrease. This finding is not surprising and reflects the new employment contract in the United States. Companies appear to want employees to be more involved in the business, but they do not want to make long-term commitments. Given this trend, it is a little bit surprising that even 5 percent of the companies said they intend to implement employment security policies.

Table 19.4, which presents the results for pay-for-performance plans, points strongly toward their increased use by the Fortune 1000. The largest increase is projected to be in the area of work-group and team incentives. This finding conforms to the growing use of self-managing work teams and the projection that they will be used more in the future. Also expected to increase substantially are nonmonetary recognition awards, individual incentives, and gainsharing. These are approaches that can create a line of sight between individual performance and reward. The plans less closely connected to controllable performance (profit sharing and stock ownership) are not projected to grow substantially.

The overall pattern of projected pay-for-performance plan adoption supports the view that organizations are trying to put in place systems that directly influence motivation and performance. This pattern is generally in agreement with what was found in 1990, although then there was more growth expected in gainsharing plans and somewhat less in work-group and team incentives. Work–team based pay is likely to continue to grow at a rapid rate, but gainsharing has somewhat peaked in popularity. Also not growing as fast as in 1990 are nonmonetary recognition awards. It is not clear why this slowdown has taken place, it may reflect the already heavy use of these awards and their success rate.

Table 19.5 presents the answer to a question concerning expected growth in TQM activities. As the figure shows, companies that already have TQM programs expect a substantial increase in these activities. This finding fits with the general high satisfaction level that organizations express with respect to their programs and with the overall trend for companies to be more concerned about the effectiveness of their management practices. It is interesting to compare this finding with that concerning quality circles. Little growth is expected in quality circles, apparently they will not be part of the general increase in total quality management activities.

Facilitators and Barriers. Installing employee involvement is a complex process. It may encounter a number of obstacles, and it needs support. Identifying critical facilitators and barriers to employee

Table 19.4

Percentage Planning Adoption/Discontinuation of Performance-Based Reward Practices.

		Completely Discontinue	Decrease Use	Stay the Same	Increase Use	Greatly Increase Use
Individual Incentives	1990	2	8	45	42	3
	1993	2	8	50	37	3
Work-Group or Team Incentives	1990	3	2	30	58	8
	1993	1	1	25	63	10
Profit Sharing	1990	2	1	71	24	2
	1993	2	3	74	18	3
Gainsharing	1990	2	0	49	45	3
	1993	4	1	57	33	5
Employee Stock Ownership Plan	1990	5	1	73	20	2
	1993	2	2	80	14	3
Stock Option Plan	1990			*— — not asked — —*		
	1993	2	4	74	17	3
Nonmonetary Recognition Awards for Performance	1990	1	1	34	55	9
	1993	1	0	43	44	13

involvement is necessary in order to gain an understanding of what it takes to implement employee involvement successfully and to gauge the degree to which it is likely to continue to be adopted.

The responses to a question concerning the degree to which a number of organizational conditions currently facilitate employee involvement activities are shown in Table 19.6. One condition stands out as an important facilitator or supporter: 45 percent of respon-

Table 19.5	Total Quality Management Change.

In the next three years, how will your corporation's use of TQM change?	
	1993 (N=213)
Greatly Decrease	1%
Decrease	4%
Stay the Same	16%
Increase	63%
Greatly Increase	15%

dents view support by top management as a great or very great facilitator of employee involvement in the organization. Support by the middle management is rated as the second-greatest facilitator, but it is rated much lower than support by senior management.

A comparison among the 1987, 1990, and 1993 responses shows a drop in the degree to which top management, middle managers, and first-line supervisors are seen as facilitators. This decline may reflect the reality that in some cases these managers lose when employee involvement programs are instituted. They often have to change their behavior significantly and may even lose their jobs because fewer supervisors and levels of management are usually needed with self-managing work teams and other employee involvement structures (Wellins, Byham, and Wilson, 1991; Lawler, 1992).

The decrease in support from top management is puzzling and worrisome. Our results show that top-management support is a particularly strong facilitator in companies identified as high users of employee involvement. In many respects, this outcome is hardly surprising, since it is hard to produce significant change in a hierarchical organization without the support of top management. There is no obvious reason why top-management support has decreased, but it may be that some feel they have already tried EI and are ready to move on to the next initiative, or it may be that they question its effectiveness. In any case, it is not a favorable condition with respect to the future adoption of EI.

Table 19.6 **Conditions Facilitating Employee Involvement.**

To what extent, if at all, is each of the following conditions currently a facilitator of employee involvement in your corporation?

CONDITIONS	Percentage Saying a Great or Very Great Facilitator[a]		
	1987	1990	1993
Support by Top Management	55	50	45
Support by Middle Management	39	26	27
Support by First-Line Supervisors	33	19	23
Availability of Resources (money, personnel, etc.) for Employee Involvement Activities	28	21	21
Business Crisis or Threat	*	*	15
Employment Security	17	9	9
Third-Party Consultation	13	15	9
Monetary Rewards for Employee Involvement Activity	7	7	6

[a] Responded 4 or 5 on a 5-point extent scale: 1 = little or no extent; 5 = very great extent; "no basis to judge" also a possible response.

* Not asked in this year.

Table 19.7 focuses on how frequently barriers are mentioned by organizations with employee involvement programs. The table shows the percentage of respondents reporting certain conditions as great or very great obstacles to employee involvement. As was true in 1987 and 1990, the condition that stands out in this table is short-term performance pressure. Much of the writing on employee involvement stresses that it is a long-term improvement approach and that it may not produce short-term results (for example, see Lawler, 1986, 1992). In addition, there can be significant start-up costs. Consultants, new staff groups, and training programs all cost money. In a business environment where quar-

Table 19.7 **Barriers to Employee Involvement.**

To what extent, if at all, is each of the following conditions currently a barrier to employee involvement efforts?

CONDITIONS	Percentage Saying a Great or Very Great Obstacle[a]		
	1987	1990	1993
Short-Term Performance Pressure	43	46	43
Lack of a Champion for Employee Involvement	26	20	25
Lack of a Long-Term Strategy	25	28	26
Unclear Employee Involvement Objectives	21	25	28
Lack of Tangible Improvements (e.g., dollar savings)	20	12	18
Worsened Business Conditions	14	14	21
Lack of Coordination of Employee Involvement Programs with Other Programs	12	17	14
Opposition by Top Management	*	*	7
Opposition by Middle Management	*	*	11
Opposition by First-Level Management	*	*	7
Lack of a Business Crisis or Threat	*	*	11

[a] Responded 4 or 5 on a 5-point extent scale: 1 = little or no extent;
5 = very great extent; "no basis to judge" also a possible response.

* Not asked in this year.

terly earnings reports are given a great deal of attention, it is not surprising that short-term performance pressures are rated as the major obstacle. This point is reinforced by the increased importance given to worsened business conditions in the 1993 results.

Overall the data on obstacles to implementation suggest that it is primarily a matter of being willing to make the commitment to producing organizational change. It is not a matter of lack of technology, knowledge, or resources. Rather it is an issue of making the commitment to a difficult long-term change process (Beer, Eisenstat, and Spector, 1990). Success requires extensive commitment on the part of employees at all levels and patience on the part of senior management. Champions are also needed to see well-developed programs through to their end regardless of short-term competitive pressure.

The data on future growth of employee involvement and total quality management programs indicate that organizations are increasingly likely to adopt them. Indeed the momentum favoring employee involvement seems to be increasing rather than remaining stable. Particularly significant is the fact that spending is expected to increase and that the programs expected to grow the most represent substantial structural changes in organizations. To be more specific, self-managing work teams, job enrichment programs, skill-based pay systems, and work-team incentives are all expected to show greater use. These programs are particularly important because they—more than some parallel participation programs—directly affect the distribution of power and rewards within a company. They are also programs that historically have not affected large numbers of employees in most organizations. The fact that their popularity is growing suggests that more and more companies are moving toward a time in which all or most employees will be in work settings where they have considerable amounts of information, power, knowledge, and rewards.

SECTION 20

Toward High Performance Organizations: Changes and Future Directions

The years since our original study of employee involvement in 1987 have been turbulent ones for many U.S. organizations. They were marked by heightened competition, organizational restructuring, downsizing, reduction of organizational layers, consolidation, and divestitures. The data in this study present a snapshot, illustrating the growing use of employee involvement and TQM practices, apparently in response to the economic challenges of the times.

In 1987, over 80 percent of companies considered themselves to have employee involvement programs, but only a few EI practices were widely used among companies and most of those covered only a minority of employees. Despite their limited use, companies consistently reported that their specific EI practices, as well as their overall EI efforts, had quite favorable effects on performance and on internal operating conditions. Most companies planned to sustain or extend their commitment to employee involvement.

In 1990, there was increased implementation of certain practices, most notably gainsharing, skill-based pay, participation groups, job enrichment, and self-managing work teams. Although the use of some practices increased, the overall coverage of the workforce by EI did not change significantly. For the most part, companies continued to be quite positive about the impact of their employee involvement practices, and most again foresaw continued investment in their employee involvement activities.

The results from 1993 in many ways continue the pattern present in the 1990 data. Increased adoption of certain employee involvement practices is quite evident. This is particularly true with respect to the increased use of self-managing work teams and a movement toward minibusiness units that allow for high levels of involvement in an overall business experience. The 1993 results also show a greater commitment to training on the part of companies but little increase in the amount of business information provided to employees. This finding quite clearly raises the question of whether employees are getting the right balance of information, knowledge, rewards, and power in order to be involved in the business.

Responses to a question asked for the first time in 1993 suggested that a small minority of the employees in the Fortune 1000 companies have a high level of involvement in them. The answers indicate that only about 10 percent of the workforce in these companies has the necessary amount of information, knowledge, power, and rewards to be involved in the business matters of their company. Overall the results suggest a continuation of the pattern that was present in 1987 and 1990: small pockets of employee involvement exist in a number of companies, but few if any companies have an organization-wide commitment.

The 1993 survey looked much more extensively at the use of total quality management practices. The results showed widespread adoption of total quality management. Over 75 percent of the companies had TQM programs. As is true with employee involvement practices, TQM programs tend to cover less that half of the workforce. Companies generally report high levels of satisfaction with their TQM programs, and they report planning to continue them. Although total quality management is a more recent phenomenon than employee involvement, the majority of companies see employee involvement as part of the total quality management thrust, rather than the other way around.

One of the most interesting and potentially important findings from the 1993 survey concerns the relationship between EI and TQM, examined for the first time in 1990. The results clearly support the argument that these two approaches and the practices associated with them are potentially complementary in their impact on organizational performance. Total quality may provide a business focus that is often missing in some employee involvement programs. A clear recommendation is that they should be treated as an integrated approach to organizational transformation. Practices that are part of each one tend to reinforce the other in a way that leads to substantially more positive results. In short, employee involvement without TQM practices is less likely to affect performance positively and vice versa. They bring important but different organization improvement practices to the change process and as a result need to be integrated.

The business motivation for adopting EI and TQM is evident in the pattern of firms that use them. Companies facing tough competitive conditions outpace the others; they appear to be involving employees to deal with very specific business challenges. Large firms report more extensive application than smaller firms. They especially use practices that have the effect of creating smaller business units for employees to focus on and feel involved in.

As did the earlier surveys, the 1993 results show quite clearly that firms consider their TQM and EI efforts to be quite successful. They also report planning to expand their EI and TQM activities.

The results strongly suggest that EI and TQM programs have a financial impact. The adoption of both EI and TQM practices is significantly related to financial performance. Firms that make greater use of EI and TQM practices have significantly higher financial performance on measures of total factor productivity, return on sales, return on assets, return on investment, and return on equity. Although we cannot prove that the adoption of EI and TQM practices will lead to improved financial performance, our data suggest this result. This is an important finding—for the first time, we see a link between the adoption of EI and TQM and the financial performance of large firms drawn from all business sectors.

The shape of organizations has changed during the last decade. Reductions in layers of management have been the result of general business conditions as well as of employee involvement. Whatever the motivation for such reductions, they have created the conditions for more extensive and profound employee involvement. Many of the more frequently used practices are those that alter the traditional logic of how firms should be managed. Such approaches as self-managing teams, skill-based pay, and gainsharing, for example, move knowledge, information, power, and rewards to the technical core of the organization and base them less on hierarchy.

The practices that have increased the most are those that move rewards and power throughout the organization. Indeed much more activity is projected in these areas. By contrast, the patterns of use and change in the areas of knowledge and information sharing are worrisome; these may end up being the factors that limit what can be attained through employee involvement. The impact of reward and power-sharing practices depends on an informed and skilled workforce. On a large scale, so does the economic strength of the nation (Reich, 1991).

Our prognosis for the future is cautiously hopeful. As with the results of 1990, we see signs in the 1993 results that companies are aligning their business needs and their management styles. They are increasingly integrating the powerful technical tools and continuous-improvement philosophy of total quality management with employee involvement. There is a slow but steady growth in practices that reshape the organization to focus more on the performance capabilities of the technical core and less on creating burdensome control structures and hierarchies.

In several respects, the glass of organizational change is half empty or half full depending upon ones perspective. Comparisons between our 1987 and 1993 results show substantial change in the way large U.S. corporations are managed, but the number of employees covered by EI-type practices remains relatively low. Most organizations are in a low-adoption position with respect to both total quality management and employee involvement.

If, as it seems likely, effective adoption of these requires not only their integration but also their company-wide installation, then most firms are failing to get the potential benefits available from a total transformation of their management practices. (In fact, for many industries, firms may still gain an advantage by being the first to complete an organization-wide transformation to a high performance approach to management.)

The data indicate that the management practices of the Fortune 1000 corporations have been and continue to be dominated by the traditional bureaucratic model of organizing. It seems increasingly likely that as a result of growing use of EI and TQM, a new approach to managing large organizations eventually will displace the traditional one. At this point, however, it is premature to argue that the dominant management approach has changed. So far the traditional bureaucratic approach has at least partially withstood the demands of a much more difficult business environment, the changing nature of the workforce, and a host of other conditions that threaten to make it an endangered species.

Research support for a transformation in management practices continues to grow. More and more studies like this one are finding that organizations that adopt TQM and EI have better financial performance. Certain institutional investors are increasingly looking at management practices as a factor in their investment decisions. Finally, government initiatives increasingly support companies moving toward employee involvement. Thus there is reason to believe that organizations will continue to evolve toward a management approach characterized by high performance work organization principles and practices.

For a large-scale change to occur, it seems likely that fundamental changes must be made in the education of the workforce so that all employees are able to handle the additional information, power, and more complex reward systems that are part of high performance organizations. A number of laws and regulations may also have to be changed so that organizations can create more egalitarian workforces and more easily share power and information with their employees. The future may show that moving to high performance work organizations is not so much an organizational as a societal change—one that can pay enormous dividends because it provides a better quality of life.

The question that remains is whether businesses can make the needed fundamental changes on an organization-wide basis. There is little doubt in our minds these must take place if organizations are to weather the storms of today and create the conditions needed for long-term viability. We believe that the outline of a new American approach to management is being defined by companies that are users of employee involvement and total quality management. This high performance management approach includes the implementation of employee involvement and total quality management practices We believe that research eventually will show that it can play a major role in helping firms be winners.

The Questionnaire

SURVEY OF EMPLOYEE INVOLVEMENT AND TOTAL QUALITY EFFORTS

The University of Southern California is conducting a survey of corporate employee involvement and total quality efforts. The purpose of this survey is to obtain information on the design, implementation, and operation of these systems. To clarify what is meant by the terms used in this questionnaire, a glossary is included.

This questionnaire is being sent to *"Fortune 1000"* corporations and should be answered by the CEO or someone who is familiar with your corporation's employee involvement and total quality efforts. Since this is a corporate wide survey, the respondent may wish to consult key staff familiar with these systems throughout the corporation. Please answer the questions in terms of **employees in the United States only.**

Your response will be kept *confidential*. The questionnaire is numbered to aid us in our follow-up efforts and will not be used to single out you or your corporation. Your answers will be combined with those of other respondents and presented only in summary form in our report. Your response is voluntary; however, we cannot make a meaningful assessment of employee involvement efforts without your help.

This questionnaire should take about 30 minutes to complete. Most of the questions can be quickly answered by checking a box or circling a number. Please return the completed questionnaire in the enclosed postage-paid envelope within *10 days* of receipt. If you have any questions, please call Edward Lawler at (213) 740-9814.

In the event the return envelope is misplaced the address is:

Professor Edward E. Lawler
Center for Effective Organizations
School of Business Administration
University of Southern California
Los Angeles, California 90089-1421

If you would like a complimentary copy of the book that reports on the results of our 1987 and 1990 surveys, please clearly print your mailing address or tape your business card below (*"**Employee Involvement and Total Quality Management**" -* Jossey-Bass, 1992):

_____

_____

_____

_____

Thank you in advance for your participation in the study.

1. **What is the title or position of the individual completing the majority of this questionnaire?** *(Check one.)*

    ☐ 1. Chief Executive Officer, Chief Operating Officer, or President

    ☐ 2. Vice President for Human Resources, Industrial Relations, or Personnel (or equivalent title)

    ☐ 3. Vice President for function other than Human Resources, Industrial Relations, or Personnel (or equivalent title)

    ☐ 4. Corporate Manager for Operations (or equivalent title)

    ☐ 5. Director or Manager of Employee Involvement or Quality (or equivalent title)

    ☐ 6. Other

2. **About how many people are currently employed full time in the United States by your corporation?** *(Please include any subsidiaries. Enter total.)*

    _____

    (Total number of employees in the U.S.)

3. **Of the total number of U.S. employees in your corporation, about what percent fall into each of the following categories?** *(Enter percents, which should add to 100%).*

1.	Hourly/clerical	_____%
2.	Technical/professional	_____%
3.	Supervisors/managers	_____%
4.	Other	_____%
	TOTAL	100%

4. **About what percent of your employees work in manufacturing operations?**

    _____%

5. **About what percent of your corporation's non-managerial employees are represented by labor union(s)?** *(Enter percent. If none, enter "0".)*

    _____%

    (Non-managerial employees represented by unions)

1

6. **On average, to what extent is your corporation's business environment characterized by the following conditions:**

	Little or No Extent	Some Extent	Moderate Extent	Great Extent	Very Great Extent
1. Subject to heavy foreign competition	1	2	3	4	5
2. Rapidly growing market	1	2	3	4	5
3. Shorter product life cycles	1	2	3	4	5
4. Declining markets	1	2	3	4	5
5. Intense quality competition	1	2	3	4	5
6. Intense speed to market competition	1	2	3	4	5
7. Intense cost competition	1	2	3	4	5
8. Rapid change	1	2	3	4	5

7. **Approximately how much has the size of your workforce changed in the last ten years?** *(Check one.)*

☐ 1. Decreased more than 50%   ☐ 8. Increased less than 20%

☐ 2. Decreased 41 to 50%   ☐ 9. Increased 21 to 40%

☐ 3. Decreased 31 to 40%   ☐ 10. Increased 41 to 60%

☐ 4. Decreased 21 to 30%   ☐ 11. Increased 61 to 80%

☐ 5. Decreased 10 to 20%   ☐ 12. Increased 81 to 100%

☐ 6. Decreased less than 10%   ☐ 13. Increased more than 100%

☐ 7. No change

8. **Has your corporation removed layers of management during the last ten years?** *(Check one.)*

☐ 1. Yes

☐ 2. No (If no, please go to the next page)

9. **If yes, how many layers of management were removed?** *(Check one.)*

☐ 1. One   ☐ 4. Four

☐ 2. Two   ☐ 5. Five

☐ 3. Three   ☐ 6. Six or More

2

This section asks questions about your corporation's information sharing, training, practices, and reward systems. (Items with an asterisk are defined in the glossary).

A. INFORMATION SHARING

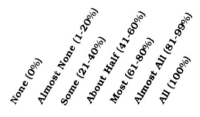

1. About how many corporation employees are routinely provided with the following types of information?

	None (0%)	Almost None (1-20%)	Some (21-40%)	About Half (41-60%)	Most (61-80%)	Almost All (81-99%)	All (100%)
1. Information about the *corporation's* overall operating results	1	2	3	4	5	6	7
2. Information about their *unit's* operating results	1	2	3	4	5	6	7
3. Advance information on new technologies that may affect them	1	2	3	4	5	6	7
4. Information on business plans/goals	1	2	3	4	5	6	7
5. Information on competitors' relative performance	1	2	3	4	5	6	7

B. TRAINING

2. About how many corporation employees have received, within the past 3 years, systematic, formal training on the following types of skills?

	None (0%)	Almost None (1-20%)	Some (21-40%)	About Half (41-60%)	Most (61-80%)	Almost All (81-99%)	All (100%)
1. Group decision-making/problem-solving skills	1	2	3	4	5	6	7
2. Leadership skills	1	2	3	4	5	6	7
3. Skills in understanding the business (accounting, finance, etc.)	1	2	3	4	5	6	7
4. Quality/statistical analysis skills	1	2	3	4	5	6	7
5. Team building skills	1	2	3	4	5	6	7
6. Job skills training	1	2	3	4	5	6	7
7. Cross training	1	2	3	4	5	6	7

3

C. PAY/REWARD SYSTEM

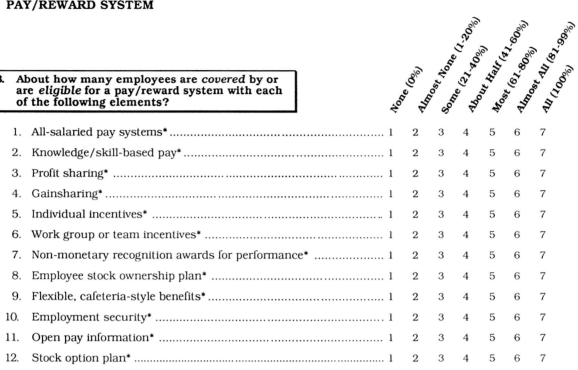

3. About how many employees are *covered* by or are *eligible* for a pay/reward system with each of the following elements?	None (0%)	Almost None (1-20%)	Some (21-40%)	About Half (41-60%)	Most (61-80%)	Almost All (81-99%)	All (100%)
1. All-salaried pay systems*	1	2	3	4	5	6	7
2. Knowledge/skill-based pay*	1	2	3	4	5	6	7
3. Profit sharing*	1	2	3	4	5	6	7
4. Gainsharing*	1	2	3	4	5	6	7
5. Individual incentives*	1	2	3	4	5	6	7
6. Work group or team incentives*	1	2	3	4	5	6	7
7. Non-monetary recognition awards for performance*	1	2	3	4	5	6	7
8. Employee stock ownership plan*	1	2	3	4	5	6	7
9. Flexible, cafeteria-style benefits*	1	2	3	4	5	6	7
10. Employment security*	1	2	3	4	5	6	7
11. Open pay information*	1	2	3	4	5	6	7
12. Stock option plan*	1	2	3	4	5	6	7

4

This section concerns types of organizational innovations or programs that some corporations have adopted in order to increase employee involvement in decisions affecting their work and work environment. You may want to consider the locations where these innovations or programs exist and then calculate the number of employees involved. Please consult the glossary insert to make sure you understand the terms.

1. About how many of your corporation's employees are currently involved in each of the following innovations or programs?	None (0%)	Almost None (1-20%)	Some (21-40%)	About Half (41-60%)	Most (61-80%)	Almost All (81-99%)	All (100%)
1. Suggestion system*	1	2	3	4	5	6	7
2. Survey feedback*	1	2	3	4	5	6	7
3. Job enrichment or redesign*	1	2	3	4	5	6	7
4. Quality circles*	1	2	3	4	5	6	7
5. Employee participation groups other than quality circles*	1	2	3	4	5	6	7
6. Union-management quality of work life (QWL) committees*	1	2	3	4	5	6	7
7. Mini-business units*	1	2	3	4	5	6	7
8. Self-managing work teams*	1	2	3	4	5	6	7
9. Employee committees concerned with policy and/or strategy*	1	2	3	4	5	6	7

5

> So far, we have asked about your corporation's use of specific employee involvement practices. Here, we ask about the extent to which your corporation uses certain *patterns* of employee involvement practices.

> 2. Approximately what percent of your corporation's employees are in units in which each of the following patterns of employee involvement practice is predominant? Please allocate 100% in answering 1-5.

_____%   1.   **None.** No significant employee involvement exists in these parts of the corporation.

_____%   2.   **Improvement Teams.** Employee involvement focuses on special groups that are responsible for recommending improvements to management. These groups may be participation groups, quality circles, quality action teams, union-management QWL committees, etc. Members of the groups receive special training to enable them to work better as a team. They receive information relevant to the problems they are working on. There may be financial rewards or recognition for team suggestions.

_____%   3.   **Job involvement.** Employee involvement focuses on creating work designs that are highly motivating, such as self-managing teams. Training focuses on job-specific skills and/or team functioning. Employees receive information relevant to their performance as individuals and/or teams. The reward system may reinforce the job design emphasis; practices might include team performance incentives or pay increases for mastering skills that are needed within a team.

_____%   4.   **Business involvement.** Employees are involved heavily in the management of the business. Improvement teams and job involvement approaches may be used as part of this strategy. Self-managing work teams and perhaps mini-business units are used extensively, and management routinely seeks employee input on policies and practices of the organization. Reward innovations are used, perhaps including gainsharing or profit sharing in the unit. Employees receive extensive training in job skills, team skills, and in business issues. Employees receive extensive business information and they are expected to use it.

_____%   5.   **Other form of involvement.** Employee involvement approaches not described by 2, 3, or 4.

> **NOTE: PERCENTAGES SHOULD ADD TO 100%**

6

> **This section asks you to evaluate reward systems and employee involvement practices and to indicate your plans for future use.**

1A. About how long has each of the following employee involvement innovations or programs been in use in your corporation? *(Enter number of years in the first column.)*

1B. How successful or unsuccessful do you think each of the following employee involvement innovations or programs is in terms of impact on improving your organization's performance? **DO NOT ANSWER FOR ANY PRACTICE YOU DO NOT HAVE IN YOUR ORGANIZATION.**

	1A. Years in Use	**Very Unsuccessful**	**Unsuccessful**	**Undecided**	**Successful**	**Very Successful**
REWARD SYSTEMS:						
1. All-salaried pay systems	_____	1	2	3	4	5
2. Knowledge/skill-based pay	_____	1	2	3	4	5
3. Profit sharing	_____	1	2	3	4	5
4. Gainsharing	_____	1	2	3	4	5
5. Individual incentives	_____	1	2	3	4	5
6. Work group or team incentives	_____	1	2	3	4	5
7. Non-monetary recognition awards for performance	_____	1	2	3	4	5
8. Employee Stock Ownership Plan	_____	1	2	3	4	5
9. Flexible, cafeteria-style benefits	_____	1	2	3	4	5
10. Employment security	_____	1	2	3	4	5
11. Open pay information	_____	1	2	3	4	5
12. Stock option plan	_____	1	2	3	4	5
INNOVATIONS/PROGRAMS:						
1. Suggestion system	_____	1	2	3	4	5
2. Survey feedback	_____	1	2	3	4	5
3. Job enrichment or redesign	_____	1	2	3	4	5
4. Quality circles	_____	1	2	3	4	5
5. Employee participation groups other than quality circles	_____	1	2	3	4	5
6. Union-management quality of work life (QWL) committees	_____	1	2	3	4	5
7. Mini-business units	_____	1	2	3	4	5
8. Self-managing work teams	_____	1	2	3	4	5
9. Employee committees concerned with policy and/or strategy	_____	1	2	3	4	5

7

		Completely Discontinue	Decrease Use	Stay the Same	Increase Use	Greatly Increase Use

> **2. Within the next 2 years, does your corporation plan to implement, continue to implement or completely discontinue the innovations/programs listed below?**

REWARD SYSTEMS:

1.	All-salaried pay systems	1	2	3	4	5
2.	Knowledge/skill-based pay	1	2	3	4	5
3.	Profit sharing	1	2	3	4	5
4.	Gainsharing	1	2	3	4	5
5.	Individual incentives	1	2	3	4	5
6.	Work group or team incentives	1	2	3	4	5
7.	Non-monetary recognition awards for performance	1	2	3	4	5
8.	Employee stock ownership plan	1	2	3	4	5
9.	Flexible, cafeteria-style benefits	1	2	3	4	5
10.	Employment security	1	2	3	4	5
11.	Open pay information	1	2	3	4	5
12.	Stock option plan	1	2	3	4	5

INNOVATIONS/PROGRAMS:

1.	Suggestion system	1	2	3	4	5
2.	Survey feedback	1	2	3	4	5
3.	Job enrichment or redesign	1	2	3	4	5
4.	Quality circles	1	2	3	4	5
5.	Employee participation groups other than quality circles	1	2	3	4	5
6.	Union-management quality of work life (QWL) committees	1	2	3	4	5
7.	Mini-business units	1	2	3	4	5
8.	Self-managing work teams	1	2	3	4	5
9.	Employee committees concerned with policy and/or strategy	1	2	3	4	5

8

This section asks questions about your corporation's employee involvement efforts. By "employee involvement" we do not mean one specific innovation and program. Rather, we refer to the full range of innovations and programs that may involve employees in decisions affecting their work and work environment.

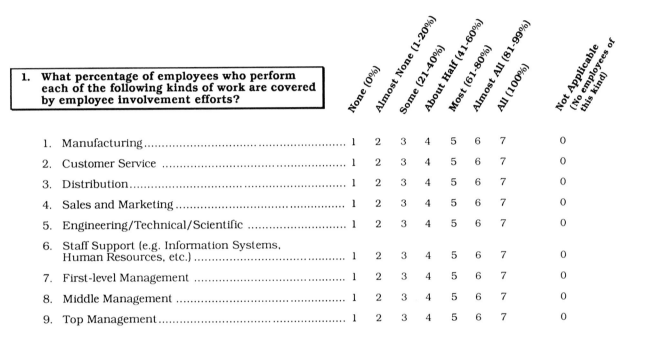

1. What percentage of employees who perform each of the following kinds of work are covered by employee involvement efforts?	None (0%)	Almost None (1-20%)	Some (21-40%)	About Half (41-60%)	Most (61-80%)	Almost All (81-99%)	All (100%)	Not Applicable (No employees of this kind)
1. Manufacturing	1	2	3	4	5	6	7	0
2. Customer Service	1	2	3	4	5	6	7	0
3. Distribution	1	2	3	4	5	6	7	0
4. Sales and Marketing	1	2	3	4	5	6	7	0
5. Engineering/Technical/Scientific	1	2	3	4	5	6	7	0
6. Staff Support (e.g. Information Systems, Human Resources, etc.)	1	2	3	4	5	6	7	0
7. First-level Management	1	2	3	4	5	6	7	0
8. Middle Management	1	2	3	4	5	6	7	0
9. Top Management	1	2	3	4	5	6	7	0

2. In the next fiscal year, do you estimate that your corporation's spending on employee involvement efforts will increase, decrease, or remain about the same? *(Check one.)*

☐ 1. Will discontinue all spending

☐ 2. Will decrease more than 25%

☐ 3. Will decrease 10 to 25%

☐ 4. Will decrease less than 10%

☐ 5. Spending will remain about the same

☐ 6. Will increase less than 10%

☐ 7. Will increase 10 to 25%

☐ 8. Will increase more than 25%

☐ 0. No basis to judge

9

3 . **To what extent, if at all, are unions involved in your corporation's employee involvement efforts?** *(Check one.)*

☐   0.   No unions (not applicable)

☐   1.   Little or no extent

☐   2.   Some extent

☐   3.   Moderate extent

☐   4.   Great extent

☐   5.   Very great extent

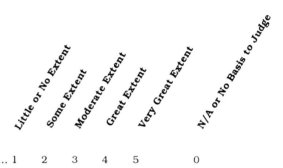

4. To what extent, if at all, is each of the following conditions currently a barrier to employee involvement efforts in your corporation?	Little or No Extent	Some Extent	Moderate Extent	Great Extent	Very Great Extent	N/A or No Basis to Judge
1. Lack of coordination of employee involvement programs with other programs	1	2	3	4	5	0
2. Short-term performance pressures	1	2	3	4	5	0
3. Unclear employee involvement objectives	1	2	3	4	5	0
4. Lack of long-term strategy	1	2	3	4	5	0
5. Lack of tangible improvements (e.g., dollar savings)	1	2	3	4	5	0
6. Lack of a "champion" for employee involvement	1	2	3	4	5	0
7. Worsened business conditions	1	2	3	4	5	0
8. Lack of a business crisis or threat	1	2	3	4	5	0
9. Opposition by top management	1	2	3	4	5	0
10. Opposition by middle management	1	2	3	4	5	0
11. Opposition by first-level management	1	2	3	4	5	0

10

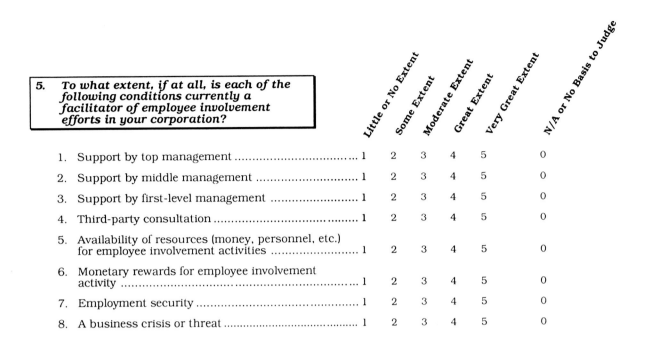

5. To what extent, if at all, is each of the following conditions currently a facilitator of employee involvement efforts in your corporation?

	Little or No Extent	Some Extent	Moderate Extent	Great Extent	Very Great Extent	N/A or No Basis to Judge
1. Support by top management	1	2	3	4	5	0
2. Support by middle management	1	2	3	4	5	0
3. Support by first-level management	1	2	3	4	5	0
4. Third-party consultation	1	2	3	4	5	0
5. Availability of resources (money, personnel, etc.) for employee involvement activities	1	2	3	4	5	0
6. Monetary rewards for employee involvement activity	1	2	3	4	5	0
7. Employment security	1	2	3	4	5	0
8. A business crisis or threat	1	2	3	4	5	0

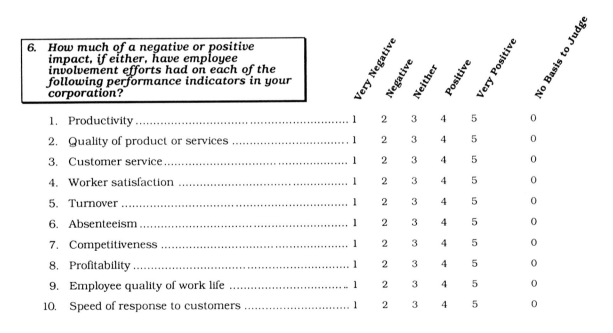

6. How much of a negative or positive impact, if either, have employee involvement efforts had on each of the following performance indicators in your corporation?

	Very Negative	Negative	Neither	Positive	Very Positive	No Basis to Judge
1. Productivity	1	2	3	4	5	0
2. Quality of product or services	1	2	3	4	5	0
3. Customer service	1	2	3	4	5	0
4. Worker satisfaction	1	2	3	4	5	0
5. Turnover	1	2	3	4	5	0
6. Absenteeism	1	2	3	4	5	0
7. Competitiveness	1	2	3	4	5	0
8. Profitability	1	2	3	4	5	0
9. Employee quality of work life	1	2	3	4	5	0
10. Speed of response to customers	1	2	3	4	5	0

11

		Little or No Extent	Some Extent	Moderate Extent	Great Extent	Very Great Extent	Don't Know
7.	**To what extent, if at all, have employee involvement efforts resulted in each of the following internal business conditions?**						
1.	Improved implementation of technology	1	2	3	4	5	6
2.	Eliminated layers of management or supervision	1	2	3	4	5	6
3.	Changed management style to one that is more participatory	1	2	3	4	5	6
4.	Improved union-management relations	1	2	3	4	5	6
5.	Moved decision-making authority to lower organizational level	1	2	3	4	5	6
6.	Moved performance-based rewards to lower organizational levels	1	2	3	4	5	6
7.	Broadened skill development at lower organizational levels	1	2	3	4	5	6
8.	Increased information flow throughout the corporation	1	2	3	4	5	6
9.	Increased employee trust in management	1	2	3	4	5	6
10.	Improved management decision making	1	2	3	4	5	6
11.	Improved employee safety/health	1	2	3	4	5	6
12.	Improved organizational processes and procedures	1	2	3	4	5	6
13.	Increased speed of decision-making	1	2	3	4	5	6
14.	Improved implementation of decisions	1	2	3	4	5	6

8. Overall how positive has your experience been with your employee involvement efforts?

☐ 1. Very Negative

☐ 2. Negative

☐ 3. Neither Negative nor Positive

☐ 4. Positive

☐ 5. Very Positive

12

1. **About what percent of employees in your corporation are covered by Total Quality Control (TQC), Total Quality Management (TQM), or similar efforts?**

_____%

(IF THE ANSWER IS 0, YOU DO NOT NEED TO ANSWER ANY ADDITIONAL QUESTIONS)

2. **In what year did TQM begin in your corporation?**

19 _____

3. **When did your quality programs start in relation to your employee involvement activities?**

☐ 1. Employee involvement started first

☐ 2. Both started simultaneously

☐ 3. Quality improvement programs started first

4. **How are they managed?**

☐ 1. Two separate programs

☐ 2. Two separate but coordinated programs

☐ 3. One integrated program

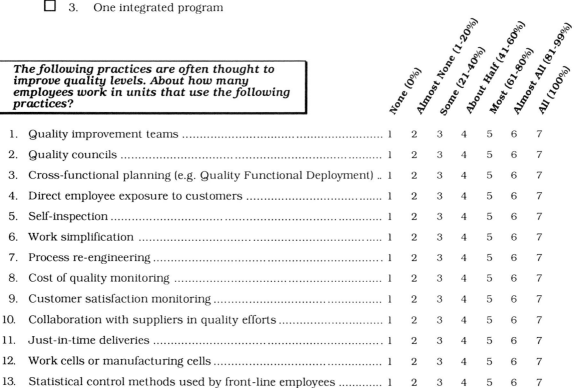

5. *The following practices are often thought to improve quality levels. About how many employees work in units that use the following practices?*	None (0%)	Almost None (1-20%)	Some (21-40%)	About Half (41-60%)	Most (61-80%)	Almost All (81-99%)	All (100%)
1. Quality improvement teams	1	2	3	4	5	6	7
2. Quality councils	1	2	3	4	5	6	7
3. Cross-functional planning (e.g. Quality Functional Deployment)	1	2	3	4	5	6	7
4. Direct employee exposure to customers	1	2	3	4	5	6	7
5. Self-inspection	1	2	3	4	5	6	7
6. Work simplification	1	2	3	4	5	6	7
7. Process re-engineering	1	2	3	4	5	6	7
8. Cost of quality monitoring	1	2	3	4	5	6	7
9. Customer satisfaction monitoring	1	2	3	4	5	6	7
10. Collaboration with suppliers in quality efforts	1	2	3	4	5	6	7
11. Just-in-time deliveries	1	2	3	4	5	6	7
12. Work cells or manufacturing cells	1	2	3	4	5	6	7
13. Statistical control methods used by front-line employees	1	2	3	4	5	6	7

13

6. **Which statement comes closest to describing how the majority of managers in your organization think about quality and employee involvement programs?**

☐ 1. Employee involvement is an important part of our quality program activities.

☐ 2. Quality activities are an important part of our employee involvement activities.

7. How much of a negative or positive impact, if either, have total quality management efforts had on each of the following performance indicators in your corporation?	Very Negative	Negative	Neither	Positive	Very Positive	No Basis to Judge
1. Productivity	1	2	3	4	5	0
2. Quality of product or services	1	2	3	4	5	0
3. Customer service	1	2	3	4	5	0
4. Worker satisfaction	1	2	3	4	5	0
5. Turnover	1	2	3	4	5	0
6. Absenteeism	1	2	3	4	5	0
7. Competitiveness	1	2	3	4	5	0
8. Profitability	1	2	3	4	5	0
9. Employee quality of work life	1	2	3	4	5	0
10. Speed of response to customers	1	2	3	4	5	0

8. **In the past 3 years, how has your corporation's use of TQM changed?** *(Check one.)*

☐ 1. Greatly decreased

☐ 2. Decreased

☐ 3. Stayed the same

☐ 4. Increased

☐ 5. Greatly increased

14

9 . **In the next 3 years, how will your corporation's use of TQM change?** *(Check one.)*

    ☐ 1. Greatly decrease

    ☐ 2. Decrease

    ☐ 3. Stay the same

    ☐ 4. Increase

    ☐ 5. Greatly increase

10 . **To what extent, if at all, are unions involved in your corporation's TQM efforts?** *(Check one.)*

    ☐ 0. No unions (not applicable)

    ☐ 1. Little or no extent

    ☐ 2. Some extent

    ☐ 3. Moderate extent

    ☐ 4. Great extent

    ☐ 5. Very great extent

11. What percentage of employees who perform each of the following kinds of work are covered by total quality management (TQM) efforts?

	None (0%)	Almost None (1-20%)	Some (21-40%)	About Half (41-60%)	Most (61-80%)	Almost All (81-99%)	All (100%)	Not Applicable (No employees of this kind)
1. Manufacturing	1	2	3	4	5	6	7	0
2. Customer Service	1	2	3	4	5	6	7	0
3. Distribution	1	2	3	4	5	6	7	0
4. Sales and Marketing	1	2	3	4	5	6	7	0
5. Engineering/Technical/Scientific	1	2	3	4	5	6	7	0
6. Staff Support (e.g. Information Systems, Human Resources, etc.)	1	2	3	4	5	6	7	0
7. First-Level Management	1	2	3	4	5	6	7	0
8. Middle Management	1	2	3	4	5	6	7	0
9. Top Management	1	2	3	4	5	6	7	0

15

12. **Are you currently competing for or in the past has your corporation competed for the Malcolm Baldridge National Quality Award?**

   ☐ 1. Yes

   ☐ 2. No (if no, skip to Question 14)

   ☐ 3. No, but plan to compete in the future (if no, skip to Question 14)

13. **Overall what was your experience with the award?**

   ☐ 1. Very Negative

   ☐ 2. Negative

   ☐ 3. Neither Negative nor Positive

   ☐ 4. Positive

   ☐ 5. Very Positive

14. **In your total quality management efforts and implementation efforts have you had significant involvement of external consultants or advisors?**

   ☐ 1. Yes

   ☐ 2. No (if no, skip to Question 16)

15. **Overall what was your experience with your consultants?**

   ☐ 1. Very Negative

   ☐ 2. Negative

   ☐ 3. Neither Negative nor Positive

   ☐ 4. Positive

   ☐ 5. Very Positive

16. **Overall how positive has your experience been with your total quality management efforts?**

   ☐ 1. Very Negative

   ☐ 2. Negative

   ☐ 3. Neither Negative nor Positive

   ☐ 4. Positive

   ☐ 5. Very Positive

16

```
┌─────────────────────────────────────┐
│ ┌─────────────────────────────────┐ │
│ │   THANK YOU FOR COMPLETING      │ │
│ │     THIS QUESTIONNAIRE          │ │
│ └─────────────────────────────────┘ │
└─────────────────────────────────────┘
```

Glossary
of Terms

Glossary of Terms

Pay/Reward Systems

1. **All-salaried pay systems:** a system in which all employees are salaried, thus eliminating the distinction between hourly and salaried employees.

2. **Knowledge/skill-based pay:** an alternative to traditional job-based pay that sets pay levels based on how many skills employees have or how many jobs they potentially can do, not on the job they are currently holding. Also called pay for skills, pay for knowledge, and competency-based pay.

3. **Profit sharing:** a bonus plan that shares some portion of corporation profits with employees. It does not include dividend sharing.

4. **Gainsharing:** plans based on a formula that shares some portion of gains in productivity, quality, cost effectiveness, or other performance indicators. The gains are shared in the form of bonuses with all employees in an organization (such as a plant). It typically includes a system of employee suggestion committees. It differs from profit sharing and an ESOP in that the basis of the formula is some set of local performance measures, not corporation profits. Examples include the Scanlon Plan, the Improshare Plan, the Rucker Plan, and various custom-designed plans.

5. **Individual incentives:** bonuses or other financial compensation tied to short-term or long-term individual performance.

6. **Work-group or team incentives:** bonuses or other financial compensation tied to short-term or long-term work-group, permanent team, or temporary team performance.

7. **Nonmonetary recognition awards for performance:** any nonmonetary reward (including gifts, publicity, dinners, etc.) for individual or group performance.

8. **Employee stock ownership plan:** a credit mechanism that enables employees to buy their employer's stock, thus giving them

an ownership stake in the corporation. The stock is held in trust until employees quit or retire.

9. **Flexible, cafeteria-style benefits:** a plan that gives employees choices in the types and amounts of various fringe benefits they receive.

10. **Employment security:** corporation policy designed to prevent layoffs.

11. **Open pay information:** a communication program that gives employees information about pay policies, ranges, increase amounts, bonus amounts, and job or skill evaluation systems. May or may not include information about what specific individuals are paid.

12. **Stock option plan:** a plan that gives employees the opportunity to purchase company stock at a previously established price.

Employee Involvement Innovations or Programs

1. **Suggestion system:** a program that elicits individual employee suggestions on improving work or the work environment.

2. **Survey feedback:** use of employee attitude survey results, not simply as an employee opinion poll but rather as part of a larger problem-solving process in which survey data are used to encourage, structure, and measure the effectiveness of employee participation.

3. **Job enrichment or redesign:** Design of work that is intended to increase worker performance and job satisfaction by increasing skill variety, autonomy, significance and identity of the task, and performance feedback.

4. **Quality circles:** structured employee participation groups in which groups of volunteers from a particular work area meet regularly to identify and suggest improvements to work-related problems. The goals of QCs are improved quality and productivity. There are no direct rewards for circle activity; group problem-solving training is provided; and the groups' only power is to suggest changes to management.

5. **Employee participation groups other than quality circles:** any employee participation groups, such as task teams or employee work councils, that do not fall within the definitions of either self-managing work teams or quality circles.

6. **Union-management quality of work life (QWL):** joint union-management committees, usually existing at multiple organizational levels, alongside the established union and management relationships and collective bargaining committees. QWL committees usually are prohibited from directly addressing contractual issues such as pay and are charged with developing changes that improve both organizational performance and employee quality of work life.

7. **Minibusiness units:** relatively small, self-contained organizational units (perhaps smaller than the plant level) that produce their own product or service and operate in a decentralized, partly autonomous fashion as a small business.

8. **Self-managing work teams:** also termed autonomous work groups, semiautonomous work groups, self-regulating work teams, or simply work teams. The work group (in some cases, acting without a supervisor) is responsible for a whole product or service and makes decisions about task assignments and work methods. The team may be responsible for its own support services (such as maintenance, purchasing, and quality control) and may perform certain personnel functions (such as hiring and firing team members and determining pay increases).

9. **Employee committees concerned with policy and/or strategy:** any group or committee that includes nonmanagement employees, created to comment on, offer advice on, or determine major corporation policies and/or business strategies.

Construction and Calculation of Index Scores

RESOURCE C

Construction and Calculation of Index Scores

Beginning in Section 5, we present results based on index scores for employee involvement and each element of employee involvement (information sharing, knowledge, rewards, and power sharing). We also present results based on index scores for total quality management. This appendix provides additional information about how the indices were constructed and calculated. Our description is aimed at interested readers who want enough information to understand our procedures, but not at academic colleagues who are interested in highly technical statistical details about the indices. The latter may contact us for more information about the measures.

Our indices of management practices are somewhat different from standard survey scales, such as job satisfaction, pay equity, or work-group conflict. These measures typically are constituted of multiple survey items. Researchers use statistical tests, such as factor analysis and internal consistency reliability analysis, to demonstrate that these items are reliable indicators of the same underlying construct. The items in the measure covary—that is, the scores on all items are highly correlated. Management practices are different because they are partly substitutable. For example, an organization that includes all employees in quality circles probably will not also include all employees in participation groups or union-management QWL committees. However, other practices, such as communication of different kinds of information, may covary as in a traditional survey scale.

Thus we created a three-step procedure to develop appropriate indices. First, we used standard statistical procedures (factor analysis and internal consistency reliability analysis) to discover practices that when combined represented different indicators of the same underlying construct. The information-sharing practices, for instance, all loaded highly on the same factor and had a high reliability score. The same is true for three social skills training items: namely, training in group decision-making and problem-solving skills, training in leadership skills, and training in team-building skills. Items with these characteristics were averaged into scales or subscales. Second, we used items relevant to each of the four major constructs that were strongly relevant theoretically and that were at least to some extent related statistically to other items in that index. Finally, we made sure that our measures of power, rewards, information, and knowledge were appropriate in all three time periods (1987, 1990, and 1993). Because we are interested in examining changes over time, we did not include in the indices items that were new in the 1993 survey. These were stock option plans and employee committees concerned with policy or strategy.

The indices reported in this book are slightly different from those we reported in our study of the 1990 data (Lawler, Mohrman, and Ledford, 1992). We dropped the weightings for some items to simplify the indices. Changes in the mix of practices companies used in 1993 led to new patterns in the relationship of practices within each index. We also revised the indices so that they would be both meaningful and consistent across all three time periods.

Employee Involvement Indices. We calculated the *information* index score for each company that was the average of the company's scores for all information-sharing practices. These are the same items that we used for the information index in previous years.

We calculated a *knowledge* index score for each firm that averaged the scores for the social skills training subscale, training in skills in understanding the business, quality/statistical analysis, job skills, and cross-training. We used all of these items in the knowledge indices we constructed in previous years, although we used a different formula for combining these items.

We calculated a *rewards* index score for each firm that averaged scores for four key reward practices that research has indicated are related both to other employee involvement practices and to organizational effectiveness. These reward practices were knowledge- or skill-based pay, profit sharing, gainsharing, and employee stock ownership plans. We dropped two items that were not used in the 1987 survey (work-group or team incentives and nonmonetary awards), one practice that research has not clearly demonstrated to impact organizational effectiveness (all-salaried pay systems), and one practice that is important but is not necessarily supportive of employee involvement efforts (individual incentives).

We calculated a *power* index score for each firm that averaged the firm's scores for survey feedback, job enrichment, quality circles, participation groups, union-management QWL committees, minibusiness units, and self-managing work teams. We dropped the use of two subscales that we used in our prior study because there was a different pattern in the data in 1993. We excluded suggestion systems from the index on statistical grounds. We excluded employee policy and strategy committees because this was a new item in 1993.

The *employee involvement* index score was obtained by averaging the index scores for each of the four constituent elements of employee involvement—that is, information, knowledge, rewards, and power. Each of the four indices was weighted equally.

Total Quality Management Indices. Our statistical analyses indicated that there were two meaningful TQM scales. *Core practices* were quality improvement teams, quality councils, cross-functional planning, process reengineering, customer satisfaction monitoring, collaboration with suppliers in quality efforts, and direct employee exposure to customers. *Production-oriented practices* include statistical control methods used by front-line employees, self-inspection, and work or manufacturing scales. Two single items did not fit with either scale: just-in-time deliveries and work simplification.

Meaning of Scale Scores. A score on any of these indices may be thought of as representing the degree of employee coverage (measured on a seven-point scale) for the average practice included in the index. The response scale for these items refers to specific percentages of employees who are covered by the practice. For example, an index score of 3.0 corresponds to the point on the scale indicating that between 21 and 40 percent of employees are covered by the average information-sharing practice. Thus the index scores have a concrete meaning.

References

References

AFL–CIO. (1985). *The changing situation of unions and their workers.* Report of the AFL–CIO Committee on the Evolution of Work. Washington, D.C.: Author.

Beer, M., Eisenstat, R. A., and Spector, B. (1990). Why change programs don't produce change. *Harvard Business Review, 68*(6), 158–166.

Blasi, J. R. (1988). *Employee ownership: Revolution or ripoff?* New York: Ballinger.

Blinder, A. S. (1990). *Paying for productivity.* Washington, D.C.: Brookings.

Bluestone, B. and Bluestone, I. (1993). *Negotiating the future.* New York: Basic Books.

Bowen, D. E., and Lawler, E. E. (1992). Facing the customer: Empowerment or production line? *Sloan Management Review, 33*(3), 31–39.

Cohen-Rosenthal, E. (1995). *Unions, management, and quality.* Chicago: Irwin.

Commission on the Skills of the American Workforce. (1990). *America's choice: High skill or low wages!* Rochester, NY: National Center on Education and the Economy.

Cotton, J. L., Vollrath, D. A., Froggatt, K. L., Lengnick-Hall, M. L., and Jennings, K. R. (1988). Employee participation: Diverse forms and different outcomes. *Academy of Management Review, 13*(1), 8–22.

Davenport, T. H. (1993). *Process innovation: Re-engineering work through information technology.* Boston: Harvard Business School Press.

Delta Consulting. (1993). *Ten years after: Learning about total quality management:* A study of CEO's and corporate quality officers of the business roundtable. Organizational Culture Series (Vol. 5). New York: Delta.

Deming, W. E. (1986). *Out of the crisis.* Cambridge, Mass.: MIT Press.

Denison, D. R. (1990). *Corporate culture and organizational effectiveness.* New York: Wiley.

Dertouzos, M. L., Lester, R. R., and Solow, R. M. (1989). Made in America: Regaining the production edge. Cambridge, Mass.: MIT Press.

Golembiewski, R. T., and Sun, B. (1990). QWL improves worksite quality: Success rates in a large pool of studies. *Human Resource Development Quarterly, 1*(1), 35–44.

Grayson, C. J., and O'Dell, C. (1988). *A two-minute warning.* New York: Free Press.

Hackman, J. R., and Oldham, G. R. (1980). *Work redesign.* Reading, Mass.: Addison-Wesley.

Hammer, M., and Champy, J. (1993). *Reengineering the corporation.* New York: Harper Business Press.

Hansen, G. S., and Wernerfelt, B. (1989). Determinants of firm performance: The relative importance of economic and organizational factors. *Strategic Management Journal, 10,* 399–411.

Herrick, N. (1990). *Joint management and employee participation: Labor and management at the crossroads.* San Francisco: Jossey-Bass.

Herzberg, F. (1966). *Work and the nature of man.* Cleveland, Ohio: World.

Hoerr, J. (1991). What should unions do? *Harvard Business Review, 69*(3), 30–45.

Huselid, M. A. (in press). The impact of human resource practices on turnover, productivity, and corporate financial performance. *Academy of Management Journal.*

Juran, J. M. (1989). *Juran on leadership for quality.* New York: Free Press.

Kochan, T. A., and Osterman, P. (1994). *The mutual gains enterprise.* Boston: Harvard Business School Press.

Lawler, E. E. (1978). The new plant revolution. *Organizational Dynamics, 6*(3), 2–12.

Lawler, E. E. (1986). *High-involvement management: Participative strategies for improving organizational performance.* San Francisco: Jossey-Bass.

Lawler, E. E. (1988). Choosing an involvement strategy. *Academy of Management Executive, 2*(3), 22–27.

Lawler, E. E. (1990). *Strategic pay: Aligning organizational strategies and pay systems.* San Francisco: Jossey-Bass.

Lawler, E. E. (1992). *The ultimate advantage: Creating the high-involvement organization.* San Francisco: Jossey-Bass.

Lawler, E. E. (1994). Total quality management and employee involvement: Are they compatible? *Academy of Management Executive, 8*(1), 68–76.

Lawler, E. E., Ledford, G. E., Jr., and Mohrman, S. A. (1989). *Employee involvement in America: A study of contemporary practice.* Houston, Tex.: American Productivity and Quality Center.

Lawler, E. E., and Mohrman, S. A. (1985). Quality circles after the fad. *Harvard Business Review, 63*(1), 64–71.

Lawler, E. E., Mohrman, S. A., and Ledford, G. E., Jr. (1992). *Employee involvement and total quality management: Practices and results in Fortune 1000 companies.* San Francisco: Jossey-Bass.

Ledford, G. E., Jr. (1991). Three case studies on skill-based pay: An overview. *Compensation and Benefits Review, 23*(2), 11–23.

Ledford, G. E., Lawler, E. E., Mohrman, S. A. The quality circle and its variations. In J. P. Campbell and R. J. Campbell (eds.), *Productivity in organizations: New perspectives from industrial and organizational psychology.* San Francisco: Jossey-Bass, 1988.

Levine, D. I. (1995). *Reinventing the workplace.* Washington, D.C.: Brookings.

Levine, D. I., Ledford, G. E., Jr., Lawler, E. E., and Mohrman, S. A. (January 1995). Employee involvement and firm performance. Paper presented at the conference on What Works at Work, Washington, D.C.

MacDuffie, J. P., and Krafcik, J. F. (1992). Integrating technology and human resources for high-performance manufacturing: Evidence from the international auto industry. In T. A. Kochan and Michael Useem (eds.), *Transforming organizations.* New York: Oxford University Press.

Mills, D. Q. (1991). *Rebirth of the corporation.* New York: Wiley.

Moran, L., Hogeveen, J., Latham, J., and Ross-Eft, D. (1994). *Winning competitive advantage: A blended strategy works best.* Cupertino, Calif.: Zenger-Miller.

O'Dell, C. (1987). *People, performance, and pay.* Houston, Tex.: American Productivity Center.

Parker, M., and Slaughter, J. (1988). *Choosing sides: Unions and the team concept.* Boston: South End Press.

Pasmore, W. A. (1988). *Designing effective organizations: The sociotechnical systems perspective.* New York: Wiley.

Pfeffer, J. (1994). *Competitive advantage through people.* Boston: Harvard Business School Press.

Porter, M. E. (1990). The competitive advantage of nations. New York: Free Press.

Reich, R. B. (1991). The work of nations. New York: Knopf.

Rogers, E. M. (1983). *Diffusion of innovations* (3rd ed.). New York: Free Press.

Rosen, C., Klein, K. J., and Young, K. M. (1986). *Employee ownership in America.* Lexington, Mass.: Lexington Books.

Schneider, B., and Bowen, D. E. (1995). *Winning the service game.* Boston, Mass.: Harvard Business School Press.

Schuster, J. R., and Zingheim, P. K. (1992). *The new pay.* New York: Lexington.

Secretary's Commission on Achieving Necessary Skills. (1991).

What work requires of schools. Washington, D.C.: U.S. Dept. of Labor.

U.S. General Accounting Office. (1981). *Productivity sharing programs: Can they contribute to productivity improvement?* Washington, D.C.: Author.

Wellins, R. S., Byham, W. C., and Wilson, J. M. (1991). *Empowered teams: Creating self-directed work groups that improve quality, productivity, and participation.* San Francisco: Jossey-Bass.

Wiggenhorn, W. (1990). Motorola U: When training becomes an education. *Harvard Business Review, 68*(4), 71–83.